THE BOTTOM LINE

Communicating in the Organization

THE
BOTTOM
LINE

Communicating in the Organization

T. Harrell Allen

Nelson-Hall nh Chicago

57175

To Carol and Maston

Library of Congress Cataloging in Publication Data

Allen, Thomas Harrell.
  The botton line.

  Includes index.
  1. Communication in management.   I. Title.
HD30.3.A43   658.4'5   78-24521
ISBN 0-88229-405-9

Manufactured in the United States of America

10   9   8   7   6   5   4   3   2   1

CONTENTS

Preface

Today it is difficult to imagine anyone whose life is not dominated by an organization. Large organizations generate the kinds of products we buy, the health care we receive, the leisure activities we enjoy, the publications we read and finally governmental agencies affect the way we live.

But you, like most of us, are affected even more directly because you earn your living by working in an organization. Within the organization you are faced with many more problems, pressures, and difficult decisions than ever before because life has grown exceedingly complex. Increasingly you must spend more time communicating with fellow workers. Often this means you must persuade them or resolve a conflict. For example, you may make a difficult decision, but to achieve your goal you must carry out the communication that goes with implementing your plans and that often proves to be the most trying part of the process. Recognizing this leads one to define management as working effectively with people and communication is essential for accomplishing things with and through others.

With this definition an organization is viewed as a maze of communication channels through which flow information, influence, power, decisions, and solutions to problems—the major activities of an organization.

This book is designed for people who work in organizations and particularly for those who supervise others. While it covers the basic activities of the practicing manager or administrator (exercising leadership and making decisions), it represents a new and significantly different approach to the study of management. Too often the traditional approach discusses abstract concepts, and ignores the actual interaction between humans, the basic, "one-on-one" situation. This book is designed to answer the pragmatist who says, "All of this talk is fine, but what do we do on Monday morning?"

The chapters deal specifically with communication in the organization. Methods for improving upward, downward, and horizontal communication, leadership and decision making, more productive meetings, effective listening and interviewing, and measuring your organization's communication climate are all discussed in detail with real world examples.

Also emphasis has been given in many chapters to self-evaluation exercises which if used as suggested will provide useful feedback on the reader's communication skills.

The editorial "he" has been used throughout the book only to avoid the more awkward and cumbersome sentence structure of "he or she."

Again this book gives the readers a view of how to survive, grow, and prosper in the organizational environment through communication. No matter how sophisticated the organization, human beings still have to make it work. People in the organization have to close the gap between goals and objectives and the chaotic realities of daily work through communicating with one another.

In the final analysis, *This Is the Bottom Line.*

Finally I wish to thank Her for making this book a physical reality. She alone knows how much she contributed.

CLOSING THE COMMUNICATION GAP

I will pay more for the ability to deal with people than any other ability under the sun.

John D. Rockefeller

Think back to the last time you attended a meeting in your organization. Did you get back to your desk confused, angry, or frustrated about what happened? Now ask yourself some questions. Did the other people listen to what you had to say? Did you listen to them? Can you recall the main points discussed in the meeting? Do you have a clear idea of what is to be done now? Did everyone understand the main ideas the way you understand them? Can you remember the conversation in detail?

If you answer no to one or more of the questions, this indicates that oral communication was not effective in that meeting. There was a breakdown in communication resulting in messages that weren't understood very well.

Motivation apparently isn't the problem. You went there with the intention of practicing effective communication. If you did, then why were there communication problems in listening, remembering, and understanding? Answers will be provided later in this book. For now, it is important to remember that good communication requires more than good intentions. Effective communication is the result of many factors working together to produce a message that is understood.

Communication in the organization is a much discussed concept. Each year millions of dollars are spent on efforts to promote better communication among people working in organizations. Why do these attempts frequently fail?

Much of the answer lies in the fact that people view communication as content rather than process. That is, they define communication too narrowly, focusing on messages, letters, memos, and orders while forgetting that the most effective form of communication is oral, face-to-face exchange between humans.

In most organizations communication generally takes two forms or styles, with one style often dominating. These styles are known as "one-way" and "two-way" communication. A one-way style results in communication flowing from the sender to the receiver. A two-way style allows the communication to flow from the sender to the receiver and back to the sender. Watching television is a common example of one-way communication. The message flows from the TV set to you, but you have no way to communicate with the announcer. Carrying on a discussion in a meeting is an example of two-way communication. Here the sender and receiver of the messages change roles constantly.

Quite often in the organization the one-way style comes to be the dominant form of communication. The likely result is communication failure throughout the organization with a loss in productivity, service, money, and morale.

As a communicator in an organization, and particularly if you supervise others, an understanding of the trade-offs between one-way and two-way communication styles is important because you can choose one over the other. You do have a choice as to how you will communicate.

Suppose that you are communicating with a group of people, coworkers or subordinates. If you select the one-way style you will be able to get your messages to them quickly saving time, but the trade off is that you will decrease the accuracy with which your message is understood, and those receiving the message will find their participation less satisfactory. If you select the two-way style, your group will tend to be more accurate in its understanding of your message. Group members will also find this style more satisfactory because they get to participate more, but the trade-off is that it will take you about twice as long to get your message through.

The longer time period is a result of feedback. That is people are able to ask questions and offer additional ideas in the two-way style.

The one-way style gives the appearance of an efficient and orderly communication climate. The messages appear to flow from the sender to the receiver with no messy questions or challenges. For example, a one-way style manager if asked if he communicated his ideas to his subordinates will likely answer, "Sure, I gave them a memo on it." The memo is a fast, orderly form of communication, but likely lacking in accuracy and satisfaction.

In the two-way style the communication is much more circular with messages flowing back and forth between sender and receiver.

It is not as orderly as the one-way, and it soon reflects the manager's skill as a communicator and even ultimately as a manager. So the two-way style produces greater accuracy and satisfaction, but it takes about twice as long as the one-way style.

For one choosing a communication style, the two-way is usually better. There are situations in which the one-way is as good or even better such as when time is more important than accuracy and satisfaction, or employees have a clear understanding of their tasks; however, in today's complex organization such instances are decreasing.

In this book I stress two-way communication. The important point for the reader to remember is that you have a great deal of control over the type of communication style you will use in your daily interaction with others. This allows you to be flexible in your communication, making your style fit the situation.

COMMUNICATION AND ORGANIZATIONAL STRUCTURE

An interesting way of looking at your organization is to view it as a honeycombed maze of communication channels through which flow information, power, decisions, and solutions to problems—the major activities of organizational life.

Such a view leads one to a novel way of looking at the organization's structure. Rather than view structure as reflected on a formal organizational chart, look at structure as actually a creation of the communication processes that are constantly on-going. For example, some people always seem to know what's going on. Sometimes you are involved in important decisions and sometimes you are not. You have noticed that if you have an important piece of information you have much more power and influence than others. And finally you may have noticed that being in the right place at the right time greatly affects what you are able to do and brings you recognition.

All of this "structure" results from communication activity, so it is important to realize that your position within the communication system of the organization determines your contributions, influence, power, promotion, and satisfaction within the organization.

Thus the resulting organizational structure based on communication stems from these exchanges: who talks with whom; how much information an individual has; how often and how much information is shared; who is often isolated from information flows; who is perceived to be the leader; the number of different people one communicates with; and one's satisfaction with his role.

COMMUNICATION STRUCTURE CHARACTERISTICS

A major difference in the way communication climates differ among organizations is whether they are "free flowing" or "restricted." This means they differ in the extent to which they allow the potential channels of communication to be used. In any organization there are numerous potential communication channels, but many are unused.

Organizations with minimal channel usage are restricted, closed structures with a minimum of exchange between employees. Organizations with maximal channel usage are open with changing structure that allows a free flow of information with maximum exchange between employees.

In some organizations the administration tends to be either centralized or decentralized. In the centralized one, a few administrators have access to many communication channels while the rest of the employees have access to only a few channels. In this structure, some positions are much more influential than others; they have greater access to information and greater inputs to solving problems. In those organizations having a decentralized administration, most positions are equal in terms of influence, access to information, and contributions to solving problems. The important characteristic is that most supervisory positions are equal. Another way of viewing these structures is that centralized and decentralized organizations tend to be "tall" and "flat", respectively.

An examination of the organization's structure reveals that some positions are more central to the organization's activities than others. A person occupying a more central position has access to more communication channels and hence more information. Closer examination reveals some positions as peripheral because of having access to few channels and information. A person in such a central role is viewed by others (particularly subordinates) as having more independence, more information, more control, and leadership.

Because of this greater access to information the person in the central role has many messages to process. This can lead to power and control, or it can result in information overload. We have all seen a person's effectiveness cut down because he simply had too much information to process. He becomes buried under an avalanche of incoming and outgoing messages. The person in the peripheral role may have too little to do, because the communication structure restricts information from getting to him. The result in some organizations is that key positions can't reach maximum effectiveness due to information overload while others have nothing to do.

Another important consideration when you are examining the organization's structure as it relates to communication activity is the complexity of the problem to be solved. With simple problems there is less need for communication channels since less information has to be processed and there is less need for interaction among employees. Usually such problems are routine and standard forms of activity can solve them. Restocking supplies, ordering new forms, and registration are examples.

However, problems do arise in the organization that are vastly more complex, thereby requiring more communication channels because more information must be processed and employees must interact more. Thus the structure must change in order to deal with this nonroutine problem.

Different types of problems generate the need for different types of communication structure within the organization. For example, suppose a novel problem is being worked on, but the solution can only be discovered if everyone shares information with everyone else. Consequently a structure is needed that opens the channels of communication, allowing the free exchange of information. In short, when high interdependence is required the structure must reflect this. On problems in which everyone working alone can ultimately solve the problem, a more restricted communication structure is sufficient because little information has to be shared. Here the employees need to interact minimally.

Finally, if employees know what the exact problem is they are to work on, or if they know what the solution must look like, they are more likely to produce. However, if either of these is known only by one or a few then a different communication structure promoting the exchange of information is needed. Management literature is full of examples of high motivation resulting from knowing how one's work helps to accomplish the overall goal. This is an important managerial technique clearly tied to communication activity because the information can be shared with everyone or kept tightly under control. Here communication exchange directly affects the potential contributions made by individuals.

From this it is obvious that an organization's structure is largely determined by communication patterns, and your place in the structure has far-reaching effects on how well you are able to do your job.

Even more important if you are in a supervisory role is to realize that you can do much to create the type of communication structure you desire. Through your own behavior you can create a one-way or two-way communication style. Even though formal communication structures may exist on organizational charts, you can have a great deal to say about how the informal or actual operating chart functions. Most tasks get accomplished through informal communication.

If you are aware that an organization's structure is created through communication by channel access, information flows, centrality of position, then you can design a structure that is best for the task you want to accomplish. Different structures can accomplish the same thing, but some do the job faster and more efficiently. Since time usually translates into money or increased service, a good manager will select the structure that allows him to get the job done most efficiently.

COMPLEXITY, ORGANIZATIONS, AND COMMUNICATION

Today's organizations reflect the complexities of the world of which they are a part. Once the neat organizational chart could have been chiseled in stone, but today the largest industrial corporations undergo a major restructuring every two to five years. This rate of upheaval is expected to increase in the organization of tomorrow.

An example of this increased complexity and frequent change is the Lockheed Aircraft Corporation when it contracted to build fifty-eight giant C-5A military air transports. In order to complete the multibillion-dollar job, an 11,000 man organization was specifically created. The management responsibilities included coordinating the work of these people as well as 6,000 companies involved in producing the more than 120,000 parts needed for each of the airplanes. But this entire organization had a planned life span of only five years when the delivery of the aircraft was completed.

While this involved a major corporation, the point is that any organization, regardless of size, is going to have increased communication problems brought on by increased complexity and frequent change.

Part of the increased complexity stems from the nature of the problems that organizations deal with today. The industrial age has passed with new types of work initiated daily. Major policies in an organization determine what products will be produced, what types of services provided, or what firms will be regulated.

An economic event occurred in 1959 to signal this age of increased complexity. The United States became the first industrialized nation to have less than 50 percent of its work force in manufacturing. This meant that nonprofit corporations, governmental agencies, and service organizations would begin to dominate the economy. Fifteen years later, about 33 percent of the work force was employed in manufacturing. Estimates suggest this figure will drop to only 20 percent by the year 2000. Today about one out of every five employees in the work force is employed by the government. By the year 2000, this figure, if current trends stay constant, will be as high as one out of three.

This change in the work force is important because manufacturing firms are less complicated than nonmanufacturing in that tasks are simpler, less information is needed by workers to do their jobs, there is less interaction among employees, and hence, the organization's structure changes little. The rule is evident, the more information an organization has to process the more structural change it will experience. If its structure is not changed and in the right way then its effectiveness is decreased. Ultimately it may even cease to exist. Because most of our organizations are nonmanufacturing, complexity in increased amounts will be the trend of the future.

Another reason for increased complexity is that today's organizations must survive in what Fred Emery and E. L. Trist term "turbulent-field" environments. Turbulent-field conditions exist when an organization has not identified the factors (let alone their probabilities of occurrence) that are necessary to its survival. This type of condition is worse than that of "uncertainty" in the industrial era when one only had to gauge market conditions of supply and demand. Here the organization knew where the ball park was and the rules of the game, but in today's turbulent environment an organization may not even know what game it is to play. This is evidenced by the deepening interdependence between the economic and the other elements of society as when an organization is caught in a web of legislation and public regulations. In short, turbulent-field environments "create" novel problems for organizations and those that work in them.

Usually organizations react to these turbulent environments inappropriately. They tend to underreact, doing nothing, hoping that conditions will change, with a resulting drop in efficiency. Or they overreact with unnecessary changes in key personnel, alterations in budgets, and so on with the result of actually adding to the turbulence.

The first signs of an organization that is attempting to operate unsuccessfully in a turbulent environment occur in communication activities. First, there are examples of communication breakdowns—"things just don't work around here any more." As the communication breakdowns and information overloads occur there will be even more specific signs: clogging of communication channels, information taking longer to reach its destination, slowed reactions to problems, new information relevant to the problems at hand never reaching the appropriate levels for proper action, more committee meetings being held and canceled, and finally certain persons no longer being as accessible as they once were.

Clearly, present and potential administrators need understanding and skill to insure the survival of their organizations and to accomplish the objectives of their organizations. They will have to prepare their organizations for increased complexity, continuous interactions with a constantly changing internal and external environment. They must clearly comprehend the many different types of structural forms—arising out of communication—that will develop in their organizations. In the development of skills to conduct planning, organizing, staffing, directing, and controlling of organizations, they must come to think as generalists and to look for common handles, wheels, and levers to guide their organizations. Usually such mechanisms of control or steering are found in the communication process or system of the organization. Throughout the development of these skills, there should be an attempt at every opportunity to improve one's communication ability.

COMMUNICATION WITHIN THE ORGANIZATION

As organizations grow in size so do their communication activities. This increased activity can mean the creation of ideas, skills, knowledge, and more human resources as people interact. But increased communicative interaction can also mean lost resources if channels become clogged.

For example, let's look at how the addition of only one more employee adds numerous chances for interaction. Suppose you are head of a small department in your organization with two subordinates. On any given work day you may be talking with one but not the other. So for each relationship there is a communication "state" of either talking or not talking, and we can calculate the total possible communication states for your department. To do this we take the number of states (talking or not talking) attached to each relationship, which in your department is just two, and then raise this to the power of the number of relationships. For three people the answer is 2^6 which gives us a total of sixty-four possible states of affairs. Now as a good effective administrator you decide to write a book of rules for controlling the communication in your department. Thus your "communication rule book" would allow for sixty-four contingencies. This would not be too hard to do and so you do it.

Then one day a new employee is added to your department making a total of four employees, just one more than your original department. Suddenly, without warning, your rule book for communication activity is no good because the number of contingencies has exploded. Now there are 4×3 or 12 relationships and 2^{12} is

4,096! If you were going to write a rule book now it would take volumes.

This little example isolates the major reason why so many organizations are in a crisis today—they fail to realize that communication controls all organizational behavior—for better or worse.

Peter Drucker makes the same point in a different way when he advises managers or potential managers to realize that management is not supervision. He says you can't supervise professional and technical people in the traditional sense. You have to figure out how to get the maximum contribution and to integrate their expertise with the organization. As the example illustrates you can't do this by writing a rule book. Drucker gives an insight on how to do this when he says that the fellow who cannot work with people is in trouble. If you can't communicate with them, you certainly can't motivate them.

Effective Interpersonal Communication

From the example of human interaction and Drucker's ideas it is obvious that an organization provides many opportunities for misunderstanding. We can conclude that the core or bottom line of administration is face-to-face communication. Research, surveys, case studies, and personal interviews indicate that a manager's total effectiveness rises or falls in proportion to his interpersonal or face-to-face communication ability.

Communication between people (it was social long before it became technological), whether it takes place in an organization or on a golf course, is basically the same. The daily difficulty of trying to understand each other is the same whether we are asking a clerk for an item or making a presentation in a committee meeting. Organization communication differs from interpersonal communication only in that the setting is different. The same basic principles apply.

Communication is simply sharing information with others. If it is effective it means shared meaning—shared understanding. An organization, full of working people, needs most of all people who can communicate. What it needs is people who are skilled at understanding people who don't explain very well and explaining to people who don't understand very well. This underscores an earlier point that two-way communication is in the long run much more effective than one-way. To be sure you are communicating ask, "How does he see it?" Don't view the communication process as starting with you—the sender. Rather view the communication process as beginning with the receiver. Chances are you are not communicating if you perceive the process as going from "I" to "you." It is much more effective if you view it as from one member of "us" to another.

Every organization has some factors that either impede or enhance the communication process. For example, departments can be so far apart physically as to make communication difficult, or if the top administrative officer is insensitive to open communication the process is hampered. Thus in the organization there are elements that impede communication over which you have little if any control. All you can do is to recognize them and try to work around them.

But the majority of the factors that affect communication are subject to your influence or control. For example, your own actions impact upon the communication process and these are largely under your control. More specifically the way you respond to a subordinate's question will have a great effect on whether he asks another question.

While there is a great deal of talk about communication in organizations, usually little is done to see that barriers are removed from the process. You may be asking yourself about now, "Yes, all of this is fine in theory, but what can I as a single individual do to induce better communication in my organization?" My answer would be that you really don't need to circulate a memo or issue orders so much as you need to create an environment which encourages two-way communication.

Any individual in any organization can have a dramatic impact on the communication process by sharpening his own skills at communicating. You can have quite an impact by realizing that you can remove many of the barriers to communication. Just reading about the communication process in an organization is a big step toward improvement. By avoiding barriers you can stop communication breakdown caused by not understanding what someone says or by having someone not understand what you mean.

An organization evolves like an onion. Its front line is its next skin, and each time it grows a new skin it becomes something else again, requiring increased efforts to keep the information flowing up and down. This may require keeping existing communication channels open or creating new ones. Unfortunately, when we operate an organization, groups of highly specialized people develop with little opportunity to interact with everyone else. What has been the result? According to management and communication consultants, more than 10 percent of U.S. businesses fail every year primarily because of bad management and ineffective communication. The chairman of the board of a multinational corporation concluded, "We have failed to create understanding among people who work together." A company president in a *Fortune* survey recently asserted, "My job is mostly talking with people." This is true of anyone supervising employees. It has been calculated that the average manager spends during his working day as much as 90 percent of his time communicating. The executive vice president of a large oil company wrote, "If I were allowed only one word to describe the primary function of a manager, I would use the term 'communicator.' "

Thus the importance of communication in the organization is established. You as an individual can do much to improve the communication process through your own individual efforts. The first step is to improve your skills as a communicator.

THE COMMUNICATION PROCESS

One of the major barriers to communication is the use of words! Words are symbols used in the communication of messages. Unfortunately different folks have different meanings for different words. True meanings are not in words, but in people. You don't really get your meaning or message across as much as you arouse that similar meaning in another person. For example, a manager might tell his foreman, "I've got a real tough problem, send me a good man." Now if the manager meant "good" to mean a cautious person concerned with details, but the foreman interpreted "good" to mean someone who was quick to act with little concern for details, a miscommunication would occur.

Thus words convey different meanings to different people, and to tell someone something is not communication. A safe rule to follow is to never assume that someone has the exact same meaning for a word that you do. For example, research indicates that 50 percent understanding between supervisor and subordinate on job descriptions is about the best level of understanding that is generally reached.

Communication is definitely more than the exchange of words. Norman B. Sigband enlarges this human activity to include the transmission and reception of ideas, feelings and attitudes— verbally and/or nonverbally—which produce a favorable response.

To really understand the dynamic, complex process of communication one must break it down and examine its parts. Basic communication models have these components: a sender and receiver, a channel, a message, barriers or "noise" in the channel, a feedback loop, and an environment in which all of this takes place. When one has experienced a communication failure you might trace the problem back through these components and see if you can identify where the error occurred. However, the communication process is greater than the sum of its parts; that is, the process requires something more than the mere addition of its components, just as a cake is more than its ingredients mixed together.

While a message can be transmitted with a great deal of technical accuracy, the receiver can only receive and decode it through his perception and experience. What he brings to the message is ultimately more important than the content for unless he can relate personally to the message its effect will be lost. Unless the message arouses in him the same meaning that it had for the encoder or speaker, the persuasive effect will be lessened. Until something is *like* something else for the receiver there is no meaning and hence no communication.

Another way to view this is to imagine the sender and receiver as large circles. Only to the extent that these circles overlap, representing similar meanings, can communication occur. If there is little overlap then there will be little understanding. Since no two people are exactly alike, there can never be complete overlap; perfect communication is impossible.

The goal then is to make those meanings overlap. This is why you were urged earlier to become receiver-centered and not word-centered. Meanings are in people, not words. Too often in communication this idea is lost. For example, Mr. One-way decides to send a message. He decides, "I'll tell Bob Jones to get that done." So he barks his message at Jones. Now Mr. One-way is satisfied that he has communicated, after all he told Jones what he wanted to say. And just to be sure, he asks Jones, "Do you understand?" Obviously Mr. Jones is going to say yes since to say anything else is to risk being viewed as a dummy by a superior. The social pressure is too great for anything but a yes. And at best an answer of yes can only mean, "I understand what I *heard*," which may be quite different from what the speaker said or meant.

COMMUNICATION AND REALITY

Since we have examined the basic elements of the communication process and stressed the need for a receiver-oriented perspective, we need to examine how our perceptions affect the communication process.

In recent years there has been a shift from viewing communication as an expression of reality to the idea that communication actually creates reality. Dr. Paul Watzlawick, prominent psychoanalyst and communication theorist, concludes, "The most dangerous delusion of all is that there is only one reality." Instead there are many different versions of reality which result from communication exchange. How else can one explain the garbled miscommunications that we see and experience daily?

COMMUNICATION FILTERS

Everyone has communication filters. More correctly we all have perceptions, attitudes, beliefs, and opinions based on experiences which tend to filter the messages we receive and transmit. Thus these filters do much to shape physical reality into our mental realities. We use communication with others to reaffirm and modify our realities. Because of this constant filtering you can't "tell it like it is." It *is* how you see it.

Studies of recent government decisions on such important topics as the Bay of Pigs, the Vietnam War, the Cuban missile crisis, and the Korean War, indicate that most of the bad decisions resulted from communication failures. That is, information was available which if properly exchanged and analyzed would have prevented many disastrous decisions.

The Bay of Pigs fiasco, for example, cannot be attributed to the lack of intellectual ability for making policy judgments. Men involved in making that decision included: President Kennedy, Dean Rusk, Robert McNamara, Douglas Dillion, Arthur Schlesinger, Jr., Allen Dulles, the Joint Chiefs of Staff and others. All of these men approved a plan based on six assumptions, each of which was wrong. How could it happen? Irving L. Janis, psychologist, attributes it to "groupthink," a mode of thinking that people engage in when they are deeply involved in a cohesive in-group. In short, the communication exchange between them created a "reality" that was doomed to failure.

Janis concludes, "Everyone becomes somewhat biased in the direction of selectively attending to the messages that feed into the members' shared feelings of confidence and optimism, disregarding those that do not."

All of us who have spent any time in an organization have seen or experienced a similar form of "groupthink."

One of the factors at work in this creation of group reality is selective perception. This means that we perceive the world or messages selectively. We attach meaning or significance to those we for some reason think important. In a group it is hard not to say something is important or significant when everyone else does. The peer pressure is tremendous. Selective perception seems to be strong when an important decision is being made. The pressure is great to join the club and be a team player. Often the negative concerns are filtered out and the decision to proceed is made.

Selective perception is constantly ongoing. Even in a simple communication event like the instant replay of a controversial call, the playback is seen differently by the respective sides.

Of the 560 advertising messages that bombard your senses

every day, you only notice about seventy-six. The rest are filtered out.

Dearborn and Simon studied a group of twenty-three executives classified as "middle management" and found that when studying a problem each executive tended to select the important "facts" as those that related specifically to the activities of his department. Another study of lower level supervisors found the same phenomenon of selective perception at work when they listed most important "facts" as those most directly affecting their department.

Selective perception works not just on an individual basis, but on the whole organization creating a portion of the communication climate. Those who work in organization engage in conversation in which some impressions are reaffirmed and others are discarded. David H. Smith concludes that certain ideas or symbols become so pervasive as to be shared by everyone, and to become part of the organization is to share these. New employees over time adopt these common beliefs with the collective "reality" of the organization transcending individual conceptions. Through a form of selective perception the employee comes to consider reality the same as his colleagues. For example, in one project it was very difficult to get employees to see that they were not in the railroad business but were actually competing in the transportation market.

Smith conducted a research study which focused on A. J. M. Sykes' theory that pictures or images of reality are embodied in myths, and he found that mythological statements are frequently used by employees to interpret organizational events. In the four organizations, varying in size, structure, and type, that were studied Smith found expressed within each common communication symbols, persistent values, and themes. Thus one measure of an organization's communication climate may be found in the common master symbols or beliefs that employees express.

In studying the communication process it is important not to forget that not only do we filter incoming information, but we also filter outgoing messages as well. There are common ways in which this filtering occurs. First, there is the tendency to simplify or shorten the message. Often we tend to simplify the message before passing it on to the next person. The communication danger here is that one may omit details that are crucial to the understanding of the receiver. Second, in our desire to convey a message that makes sense we may add details. No one wants to send a message that appears to be incomplete so there is a tendency to add details before passing it along. The danger comes from the fact that we may add details that are not true and thus distort the message. Third, since no one likes to bring the bad news there is a tendency to downplay its importance particularly when informing a superior. From an organizational perspective as bad news moves up the organizational ladder, it tends to lose its harshness or unpleasant elements. We've all experienced the boss who screams upon learning of the bad news, "Why wasn't I told about this sooner."

THE IMPORTANCE OF FEEDBACK

One of the best ways to overcome the natural filtering process and to become an effective communicator is to learn to rely on feedback.

One begins by being receiver-oriented. What you need are reactions by the receiver to your message. You can stimulate reactions by asking, "What do you think about that?" or "Why do you think that?" Simple questions but how often have you heard them lately? You want to use this type of question to generate feedback so you can measure the effectiveness of your message.

Feedback is a term borrowed from cybernetics. In a technical sense it refers to the ability of man and certain machines to detect error or deviation from what is the goal, and then "feed back" that error to a control mechanism, which then makes the necessary correction. An automatic pilot on an airplane is a common example. In human terms the concept refers to the sender getting a favorable response from the receiver which indicates that the goal of understanding has been met.

Not only should you try to get feedback on your own messages, but you should also give feedback when ideas or questions are presented to you. Suppose a subordinate comes to you and asks for a raise. The employee has carefully prepared his reasons and begins to make his case. To be sure that you really understand his arguments you may repeat part of his message from time to time and when he has finished ask to summarize his position. If you can do this successfully you will have accomplished two immediate goals. You will have eliminated the chance that filters have distorted the communication, and you will have established some rapport with your subordinate regardless of your final decision. If you must say no, you will have taken some of the sting out of it for him by communicating that you at least listened to him with understanding.

Sensitivity to feedback can be learned through practice. The first step is to realize that it exists and that it is crucial to effective communication. The next chapter on nonverbal communication will give additional insights to feedback cues.

Anthony Jay writes about the importance of feedback to the administrator or manager on a different level. In discussing the nature of the leader, Jay refers to the feedback loop as the "raw nerve." If working properly, this nerve should pick up even faint signals that something is not working properly: the slight irritation in an important customer's voice, a bit of conversation among employees, a question concerning policy overheard in an elevator, or a sales figure that is slightly down. Jay concludes the successful leader must keep his feedback nerve as raw and sensitive as possible because a deadened feedback nerve is usually the prelude to a disaster.

COMMUNICATION BEGINS WITH YOU

Communication must become an integral part of management. It must be considered as important as profit and productivity because it directly affects both. In too many organizations effective communication is taken for granted.

A dramatic example of the turnaround that an improved effective communication climate can make is the recent upsurgence of Chrysler Corporation's share of the British market. Just eight months after the operations were saved from liquidation, production ran 30 percent ahead of target, strikes were cut to one fifth of the previous year's level, laid-off workers were recalled, and Chrysler had increased its share of the market from a rock bottom 5 percent to 7.9 percent. Chrysler's chairman, John Riccardo, ordered his British managers to change their attitude toward labor and improve communications on the shop floor. One example of this was the invitation to sixteen shop stewards to meet monthly and discuss work performances and production goals with top plant officials. One of the shop stewards summed up the rapid transformation by saying, "Management began to treat us like men, like adults." Chrysler president Eugene Cafiero said, "There's a new spirit of working together."

This real world event underscores one of the perplexing facets of human communication: sometimes it is so simple and at other times so hopelessly complex. What appears to be a technological problem easily solved soon turns into a crisis because the human element was ignored. A current survey of administrators reveals that 55 percent claim they still have to rely on the grapevine for information about their problems and organizational policy.

If your organization is to become effective, you are going to have to learn how to communicate and work at communication. This book is designed to help you close your current communication gap.

USING THE SILENT LANGUAGE: NONVERBAL COMMUNICATION

You cannot not communicate.

Paul Watzlawick

The executive's skill was always equal to his reputation. His personal style, developed through years of learning and practice, was to badger, intimidate, overwhelm his opponent into submission. As the executive moved in close to his victim, so close the opponent would inevitably back up, his heavy eyebrows would rise and fall in harmony with his booming voice. He took great pride in his reputation of never losing a face-to-face encounter.

By contrast a female executive had a blue carpet installed in her office, the furniture covered in blue corduroy, and the walls, even the venetian blinds, painted blue. Her secretary sat in a blue chair and typed on, what else, a blue IBM Selectric II with a blue ribbon. The increase of the woman's power could easily be traced by the blue filing cabinets, desks, floors, coffee mugs, and water coolers. Michael Korda in his best-selling book, *Power*, details how the color had its impact. The people who worked for this executive soon began wearing blue to match their environment, and the heads of other departments, threatened by the symbolic power of the color, trembled when their secretaries turned up for work in blue dresses.

Both of these executives knew how to use nonverbal communication to their advantage. In many ways nonverbal is more important than verbal communication. Only 7 percent of a message's effect is carried by words, and the listener receives the other 93 percent through nonverbal means. However, while each of us has probably studied verbal communication, both written and oral, we may not have been trained in understanding nonverbal communication.

If you made a written transcript of a conversation you recently had with your superior, would that written document fully communicate the total picture of what happened? Obviously not. While you were listening to your superior, all of your senses were acutely working. Information was being processed about his intonation, facial expressions, posture, word choice, dress, and countless other things. Taken together all of this input made your final impression of the meeting.

A salesman leaves a client after a detailed discussion of an order, but without receiving the decision of the client, he returns to his company. He tells his supervisor that he feels confident the sale will be made. Why? Each of us goes through our daily routine "reading" nonverbal cues. It has even been suggested that those who are most successful have learned how to avoid betrayal by nonverbal contradictions.

Every day in the organizational world, people reveal their status and power by their nonverbal communication. It may happen when an individual insists that his companion go through the door first or when an individual strides through the door ahead of his group. When individuals enter the room and seat themselves for a meeting, their selection of seats communicates who has power and who doesn't. By observing the objects and order of a fellow employee's office, certain conclusions can be drawn about him.

All of this communication gives us insights into the behavior and perceptions of ourselves and others. By being aware of nonverbal communication, we can more accurately understand what is going on around us.

Three important principles of nonverbal communication detailed by Jim D. Hughey and Arlee W. Johnson are: (1) We cannot not communicate. (2) Nonverbal communication deals with feelings and attitudes. (3) Nonverbal messages are thought to have high credibility.

To avoid speaking is not to avoid communicating. Silence itself communicates. Thus, Paul Watzlawick, Janet Beavin, and Don D. Jackson phrased the axiom, "You cannot not communicate." This impossibility of not communicating is extremely important because it means that each of us is a kind of transmitter which cannot be shut off. No matter what we do or don't do, we are sending out messages that say some things about ourselves. In the same way, the people with whom we work are constantly giving out information about themselves.

Nonverbal communication transmits feelings. When we are trying to determine the state of a person's mind, we usually rely on nonverbal cues. For that reason some business, such as negotiations, is best conducted face to face rather than by telephone. Important nonverbal cues are missed unless you can actually observe the person's reactions. Nervousness, tension, and anxiety are always conveyed by nonverbal communication. Most of the information we use in determining a person's attitudes or feelings does not come from the words he uses, but from what has been referred to as the "silent language."

Nonverbal messages have high credibility. "Actions speak louder than words" is an age-old proverb, but recent nonverbal research confirms it—when information communicated nonverbally contradicts information communicated verbally, the nonverbal communication is generally believed. Why? Because most of us agree that we cannot control our nonverbal cues as well as we can control our words. At one time or another we have all been deliberately misled by the words used, not by the nonverbal communication which accompanied them. Actually the individual sensitive to reading nonverbal cues often can tell when a contradiction between the nonverbal and verbal exists. This mixed communication is resolved in favor of the nonverbal. If you enter a client's office and he greets you, "Glad to see you," but he accompanies that statement with an expressionless face and a limp handshake, what do you conclude?

Nonverbal communication can be divided into three categories: environment, body movements, and voice. The environment can communicate through time, space, architecture, color, furnishings, and objects. People can communicate through the use of their bodies and physical behavior. Messages can communicate through various manipulations of vocal tone, rate, pitch, and volume.

THE ENVIRONMENT

In considering how the environment communicates, recall for a moment the different offices you have visited lately. Some of these offices were probably more comfortable than others. Of course, your impression was influenced by the type of business pending and the person you were meeting, but let's focus on the office. Was it extremely formal? What made it seem so stiff and cold?

There's a large amount of research which shows that the design of an environment can influence the kind of communication that takes place in it. The attractiveness of the room, for example, influences the happiness and energy of the people working in it. In one experiment at Brandeis University three rooms were used: an "ugly" one, which resembled a janitor's closet in the basement of a campus building; an "average" room, which was a professor's office; and a "beautiful" room, which was furnished with carpeting, drapes, and comfortable furniture. Results of the experiment showed that while in the ugly room, the individuals became tired and bored more quickly and took longer to complete their task. When they moved to the beautiful room, however, they showed a greater desire to work, and expressed feelings of importance, comfort, and enjoyment.

Depending on the type of business, the environment can be used to prolong the customers' stay or hurry them on their way. A quick food carry out keeps the lights shining brightly and the noise level high. On the other hand, a nice restaurant is dimly lighted, and the noise level is very low. Airports with their uncomfortable chairs bolted to the floor encourage people to escape to the quiet bars and restaurants where they will spend their money.

Since the environment directly influences the amount and kind of communication that takes place in it, the sensitive communicator in an organization must be aware of territory and space, color, office furnishings, and arrangements and objects.

TERRITORY AND SPACE

The way people use territory and space can communicate a great deal about power and status relationships. Edward T. Hall, an anthropologist, concludes that all people lay claim to and defend a particular territory. This "claim" in an organizational setting refers to those personal objects an individual uses to communicate that this territory is his. In the largest room of typists' desks, each has something which uniquely converts that grey, steel object into "hers."

Anyone who doubts the importance of man's instinct to have his territory reflect his view of reality need only to consider that in the last decade this principle was demonstrated by the deaths of several thousand young Americans. During 1968, the United States, South Vietnam, and North Vietnam spent eight months arguing over the size and shape of the table at which they would hold their peace talks. The concept of territoriality was of primary importance. The North Vietnamese wanted a square table which would have given the National Liberation Front (NLF) guerillas a separate side all to themselves. The United States was opposed to that design and proposed two rectangular tables, one seating themselves and the other for the North Vietnamese and NLF. The ultimate solution, months later, was a round table which, having no sides at all, allowed each side to claim victory.

Gerald M. Goldhaber has identified three principles relating to territory and status in an organization. Personnel with high status will usually (1) have greater territory; (2) protect their territory better; and (3) invade the territory of lower status personnel.

Could you look at the blueprints of a collection of offices and determine the status of the occupants? Probably so. There are several rules about office locations: the higher up, the better; the bigger, the better; and the corner office is best of all. In his book on how to get power, Michael Korda describes "a corner power system." Power tends to communicate itself from corner to corner in an X-shaped pattern, leaving certain areas as dead-space in power terms, even though they may contain large and comfortable offices with outside windows.

Korda cites the extreme example of a man who managed to obtain a corner office by the age of fifty. Once there he decorated his office with photographs of his children and frequently played golf. Eventually his authority within the corporation declined—he was no longer invited to meetings, cash-flow reports no longer appeared on his desk, and he was taken off the office distribution list for information reports. Nevertheless he kept his office, located at one of the four poles of power, until he retired at the age of sixty-five.

Proximity to power is the second best thing to having a power spot to call your own. Power diminishes with distance. Post someone's assistant next to his superior's office, and he benefits from being close to the source of power. Promote the assistant to a larger office that is further away, and his power is likely to decrease. An administrative assistant for the head of a state agency had a desk situated in a hallway between the chief executive's office and the deputy director's office. For three years he occupied that territory, and when he left, it was to head his own division. His division offices were located down the hall from the chief executive's but were separated by a series of four elevators. When a new state building was erected, he led the fight for justifying the division's need for additional office space. When the move was made, where was his division suite located? Adjacent to the chief executive!

The second principle Goldhaber cites is that high status individuals protect their territory better. The more important a person is the less accessible he is. Obviously you cannot call the President of the United States and expect to get him on the phone nor can you drop by the White House for a friendly chat. A person with high status is usually very well protected. For example, the executive suite of a large research and development organization is divided from the regular hallway by two massive oak doors. The painted walls are replaced by expensive paneling, the floor covered by a deep plush carpeting. The outer office is guarded by a receptionist. Once past this obstacle the visitor is ushered into the director's suite which is protected by his private secretary. When the visitor enters the director's office, he will most likely find him behind a desk which is located so that he can quickly glance up and see who is coming in the door.

Albert Mehrabian, a psychologist, explains that a clue to status differences is the degree of hesitation and discomfort shown by the visitor as he gets closer to the person he visits. The greater the difference, the longer the low status individual waits before making any move to come closer. He sits only when invited, and then as far away as possible.

The third principle of high status personnel is that they freely invade the territory of those with lower status. When was the last time you complained about your boss casually dropping in your office? Thus, territory is a reflection of status. Those with more status "control" space and those with less respect it.

Research shows that a man's status can be identified by spatial relationships. Viewers watched a film which depicted a man who knocked on an office door, entered, and approached a man seated at a desk. The caller was consistently rated subordinate if he stopped just inside the door and conversed from that distance with the man at the desk. Time between the knock and the man at the desk answering was also related to status—the longer it took the man to respond to the knock, the higher his status was judged.

When an individual expects praise he tends to sit closer to his superior than if he expects to be reprimanded. Thus, space can act as a defense. In much the same way, we stand closer to someone we perceive to be friendly than to an unfriendly person.

Anthropologist Edward T. Hall identified what he termed informal space. Informal space is carried with each of us and expands and contracts depending on the circumstances—the type of encounter, our relationship with the persons, and many other factors. Hall concludes that we choose one of four different distances depending upon how we feel toward the other person at a given time. By being aware of these distances, we can "read" the distance a person takes and get some insight into his feelings.

The first of Hall's distances is termed *intimate*. It begins with skin contact and ranges out to about eighteen inches. By allowing someone to move into our intimate distance we're letting them enter our territory. This is a sign of trust. Occasionally circumstances will demand that a stranger invade this distance, such as on crowded buses and elevators. Our usual defense is to look away, avoiding eye contact. This signals that we are not invading by choice but necessity.

The second informal distance is the *personal zone* of from eighteen inches to four feet. The executive who liked to intimidate through face-to-face encounters used this distance effectively. As he approached his main point, he would lean toward his opponent in a threatening way.

Social distance, from four to about twelve feet, is the distance at which most business transactions occur. Conversations and discussion normally occur from four to seven feet among people who work together. An indication of how you feel about the people with whom you work could be the distance at which you feel comfort with them. For example, a man whose reputation with the company was good had been accustomed to sitting near his superior's desk when discussing a problem. However, when the man resigned to join another firm, suddenly he found the distance he was allowed had increased from four feet to ten feet. Normally ten or twelve feet is the range at which we sit from our superior who is usually seated behind his desk. By keeping the barrier of the desk between you, the boss is indicating that he is in a "one-up" or superior power position.

Hall's farthest zone begins at twelve feet and extends outward to the limits of visibility or hearing. These distances are reserved for the speaker who is addressing a large group. One corporation had an annual meeting every spring for professional employees. At this meeting the corporation president and vice presidents made a progress report on how the year had been. After their presentation, they called for questions from the audience, but there were none. The president always bitterly complained, "Why won't employees ask questions? Don't they have any interest in the company?"

Finally a vice president pointed out that the microphone was located in front of the first row of spectator seats. As the questioner would address the president, he would look up at him on the stage, protected behind a large oak podium. To the president's right a male executive secretary would be making a transcript of the questioner's name, question, and the president's response. It was not at all surprising that this threatening atmosphere inhibited employees from leaving their seats!

COLOR

Some specific colors have been associated with various human "moods." As a result, the color of an office can communicate. Many offices are painted blue which is associated with being secure, calm, and powerful. By comparison, yellow is considered cheerful, jovial, and many think perhaps too frivolous for the office of a successful professional. Beige or tan are neutral colors and thus not impressive. Since color establishes the visual environment, executive color consultants analyze the businessman's character and appearance to find the colors most appropriate for him.

The color selection not only applies to his office walls, but is often used as the basis for an entire new wardrobe. When Gerald Ford took office as President he was photographed wearing colorful, striped ties. Soon those ties disappeared and were replaced by ones in conservative colors, with small patterns. It was suggested that such neckwear was more appropriate for the Chief Executive of the United States.

Color is often used in offices to identify who controls the space. The female executive's use of the color blue cited at the beginning of this chapter is an excellent example of this. Color indicates possession of the territory.

Often the color of a room affects the type of communication that takes place there. According to Goldhaber, warm colors (yellow, orange, red) apparently stimulate creativity and make people feel more outgoing while cool colors (blue, green, gray) encourage deep thought processes and may inhibit both the frequency and quality of communication.

OFFICE FURNISHINGS AND ARRANGEMENTS

Whenever you enter a private office, there are two levels of nonverbal communication which give off information about the person who occupies that office. The first level is the furnishings themselves and the second level is the arrangement of those furnishings.

The importance of the man or woman's position in the organization can be surmised by evaluating the furnishings. Is the office carpeted? Is it paneled? Is there a private bathroom? The higher up in the organization the more likely the desk is wood rather than metal and the desk chair to be high back rather than standard. Completing the furnishings are bookcases, a work table, and a credenza. The executive's office comes complete with the home furnishings of a sofa, coffee table, easy chairs, and art work.

Although filing cabinets are generally regarded as a nuisance to be hidden in a corner of the secretary's office, they can take on significance, especially when decorated with a huge lock. This communicates that whatever is contained in the filing cabinet is terribly important and thus reflects on the importance of the person who is trusted with their keeping. In a research and development organization, locked filing cabinets abound, and many are locked with a massive iron bar which slides through the drawer handles.

These are high status since they communicate not only that important documents are inside but that they are top secret!

Filing cabinets can be used in an outer office to contribute to the atmosphere that highly significant work is done by the people located within. A midlevel administrator completely redesigned his offices so that when a visitor came in the door he was facing a wall of filing cabinets. His secretary was protectively positioned in front of them—like a guard. Since the filing cabinets were located adjacent to his office and his secretary was protecting them, the assumption was that all contained his work. In reality, only two were his and the remainder had been pulled from the offices of subordinates under the thinly veiled pretense of setting up a central filing system.

More important than the furnishings of an office, however, is the arrangement of those furnishings. In his study of the communication of power, Michael Korda discusses how the office arrangement is used to put the visitor at a disadvantage. In a large office the visitor has to walk the length of it before getting to the desk and as many objects as possible—coffee tables, chairs, and sofas—are used to slow his progress. The ideal arrangement for any office, regardless of size, is to have the visitor's chair facing toward you, so that you are separated by the width of your desk. The desk in a small office should be placed well forward in the room, thus minimizing the space available for the visitor.

In larger offices the arrangements are more varied. There are generally two separate sections, one containing a couch which can be used for informal, semisocial discussions and the other containing the desk and chair. The semisocial area is used when decisions do not actually have to be made, and the more traditional desk and chair can be used when a decision must be reached. Thus the areas are referred to as the semisocial area and the pressure area. Which area the visitor is seated in becomes a clue as to the type of discussion to take place.

The use of the office arrangement can be a reflection of the administrator's attitude. When the employee approaches the superior with a complaint, the superior who stays behind his desk is communicating his one-up authority and is likely to be unsympathetic whereas the superior who chooses to sit in the semisocial area (from behind the desk) is likely to be more open and receptive.

In a study conducted in a doctor's office it was found that desk placement had a significant effect on the tension experienced by the patient. When the desk separated the doctor and patient, only 10 percent of the patients reported themselves at ease. That percent jumped to 55 when the desk was removed from between them. This indicates that the desk acts as a barrier to communication.

Certain administrators, fully aware of this, use the desk in that way. Others deemphasize the desk by moving it to a less conspicuous location. The executive who values more open management may place the front of his desk against the wall. This lessens the status difference between superior and subordinate and increases the conversation. The manager appears more open and accessible to anyone entering his office.

The office furnishings and their arrangement communicate the importance of the individual and his priorities. Few things in an office are left to chance, rather they are strategically placed by design. If you spend an entire meeting looking up at your opponent from a low chair, blinded by sun from the window, your discomfort is not an accident. The ashtray left just out of your reach was probably placed there to increase your awkwardness. On the other hand, a meeting between two individuals without the barrier of the desk can go very smoothly and be highly productive. It depends on the attitude, goals, and priorities of the occupant of the office. By understanding the use of nonverbal communication, you will be better able to determine what those are.

OBJECTS

In addition to the furnishings of an office, there are any number of objects which nonverbally indicate the status of the individual. Of course, these vary from organization to organization and what was once a status symbol may have been replaced by something else. For example, the key to the executive's washroom once rated high on the list of status objects which communicated prestige, but with increasing numbers of women occupying important positions its significance has diminished.

Of course, the ultimate object is the limousine which instantly communicates that the occupant is successful, powerful, and wealthy. A visitor to Washington, D.C., remarked with amazement, "Is everyone in this city important?" He was reacting to the numerous sleek, black limousines which populate the capital.

Particularly in cities where parking is a constant problem the private parking space is highly valued, and the closer to the building the better. In large corporations where all employees are required to wear name tags for security purposes, the tags are often distinguished for status purposes.

In a research and development organization the color of the tag reflected the individual's security clearance. Naturally only the more important employees enjoyed a top secret clearance so the colors became an indication of status level.

Most large corporations have an object which has importance within that organization. It may be a particular kind of clock, gold plated thermos bottle, a type of painting, or style of telephone. Anyone familiar with the organization can identify the object and interpret its meaning.

TIME

In understanding the communication of time there is one universal rule: the more important one becomes, the more valuable his time must appear to be. Consequently a meeting with an executive confers status on the subordinate by communicating that he is important enough to get some of the executive's highly valuable time.

The most obvious game involving time is who schedules the meeting and who arrives last. If a manager sets a meeting for 10:30, you can bet he will still be in his office at that hour regardless of how far away the conference room is located. A meeting for raising funds for a worthy social cause was held in Detroit. The public relations men for two large competing automobile corporations were to attend. Since one of the men was to chair the meeting, it could not begin without him. Arriving thirty minutes late, he rushed into the room, explaining how a "crisis" had delayed him. Meanwhile his public relations opponent, having discovered upon his arrival that the chairman had not yet arrived, excused himself to go to the men's room. The chairman, discovering his opponent was not in the room, quickly added that his "crisis" required one more phone call and then he would begin the meeting. While the other committee members waited another thirty minutes, the two men jockeyed for position of arriving last. Since the phone and the bathroom door were near each other, the public relations man emerged to see the chairman on the phone, and he too decided to call his office from an adjacent phone. After much conversation with no doubt puzzled secretaries, both men, perceiving the deadlocked contest, hung up and walked into the meeting together.

These same tactics are used by administrators when they are meeting someone for lunch. Always the person who arrives last is in a one-up position. It is not a coincidence that all the phone booths around a nice restaurant are full at lunch time. They are populated by men and women who are maneuvering to arrive last!

The most obvious communication of time is the person who deliberately checks his wrist watch—a sure indication that your time is about up. Another way of emphasizing the importance of one's time is the use of clocks. A clock in an office is itself a communication signal that the occupant's time is valuable. The size of the clock and the direction it faces also communicate. Large clocks which have a moving pendulum and face the visitor indicate that time is quickly passing and is not to be wasted.

PHYSICAL APPEARANCE

Research indicates that as early as age three teachers show preference for those children who are cute and muscular. Certainly as one progresses through life the preference for slender, attractive people only increases. Americans particularly have always been drawn to the muscular physique. Diet books of all kinds continually rise to the top of the best-seller list as thousands search for a magic formula to trimness and beauty. One's physical appearance communicates certain things about him. This can be divided into clothes, hair, and personal adornments.

What do your clothes tell others about you? While clothes may not "make the man" as advertisers would have us believe, they do influence the way in which others perceive us. The most obvious example of clothes that communicate is the military uniform which tells the individual's organization, rank, job, and perhaps years of service.

We are most influenced by the clothing of strangers in making judgments. For example, a British study showed that middle-class subjects disclosed significantly more personal information to a market researcher when he was wearing a tie than when he was not.

A man who has preached the importance of clothes in the organization is John T. Malloy, America's first wardrobe engineer. Malloy offers a number of courses designed to teach clients how to dress more effectively. He teaches "an upper-middle-class set of color and pattern values" designed to help boost the client's career in the corporate world. He also does an extensive study to determine how to best project a desired image. One of his successes is the owner of an insurance agency who replaced his flashily attired sales force with men in gray suits and simple ties. The result—sales boomed!

Everyone has an opinion on hair—not only their own but everyone else's as well. The emotions accompanying opinions on hair were frequently illustrated in the late 1960s. The placement officer of a large western university concluded in 1971 that job opportunities for males were found directly proportionate to the length of their hair. The longer the hair, the fewer the jobs. While this attitude has lessened somewhat in recent years, most organizations still prefer short hair on male employees. Mustaches have gained in popularity, but some executives still prefer their employees to be clean shaven.

Indications are that a man with a beard is considered threatening. Although women attribute such characteristics as "masculine," "sophisticated," and "mature" to a beard, men prefer to stand closer to beardless men. Even men who have beards themselves, according to D. G. Freedman, are less tense with unbearded male strangers than with other bearded men. The bearded executive or top administrator remains a rarity.

In addition to clothes and hair, an individual can use personal adornments to communicate something about himself. Employees given pins to recognize their years of service will wear them only when the pin truly distinguishes them, such as for twenty-five years service. Glasses have long been regarded as indicative of high intelligence and industriousness.

FACIAL EXPRESSIONS

Facial expressions are generally regarded as a means of nonverbally communicating one's emotions. Most Americans, however, are not likely to be too expressive in their facial behavior. Particularly is this true in the organizational setting. The social rules generally require the masking of emotional reactions—an extremely angry man tries to present a neutral face and an unhappy person is allowed only a hint of downturned lips.

Since each of us is aware that our face can "give us away," we try to control what information it sends. This control leads to the intentional display of a particular face. When you are trying to read someone's facial expression, look for expressions that seem to be overdone. Often the person who is pretending an emotion he does not really feel tends to exaggerate the expression. Another way to detect a person's feelings is by watching his expression at moments when he isn't likely to be thinking about his appearance. We have all been asked to read a memo or letter and have felt the person's eyes studying our facial expression. A better strategy is to ignore obvious gestures and then try to glance at the more true facial expression.

What makes face reading difficult is the ability of the face to convey multiple emotions rather than a single emotional state. Additionally, an emotion can be shown on the face for as short a time as one-fifth of a second. According to Mark Knapp, the evidence on facial expressions seems to show: (1) the best predictors for "happiness" are the lower face and the eye area; (2) the eyes are most revealing for "sadness"; (3) the eye area and the lower face tell us most about "surprise"; (4) "anger" is best identified by the lower face and the brows and forehead; (5) the lower face is the best predictor for "disgust"; and (6) "fear" identifications seem most heavily weighted in the eye area.

Thus the complexity of the human face makes it difficult to read accurately. Each of us has learned to mask our emotions with appropriate expressions. This has caused many people to focus their attention on the eyes which supposedly "cannot lie."

EYES

Eyes can be used to invite, ask, intimidate, threaten, or hide. When one wants to indicate the need for involvement or inclusion, he uses his eyes. On the other hand, a person can use his eyes to produce anxiety in others. We have all experienced the "cold stare" and by looking down or away have indicated submission to it.

Just as eye contact can be used to communicate, no eye contact can also convey meaning. It is absent when people want to hide something concerning their inner feelings, or when an individual does not desire social contact with a certain person or persons. In highly competitive situations, when there is dislike or tension, the people usually will not look at one another.

Representatives from two well-known management consultant firms were once seated directly opposite each other in an executive's outer office while waiting to make their presentations for an important contract. Although there was a long wait before one of the men was called to make his presentation, neither man looked at the other the entire time.

Another important function of eye contact is regulating conversation. Have you ever had difficulty talking with someone wearing sunglasses? During the everyday exchange of words, while people focus their attention on what is being said, eye movements notify each person when it's his turn to talk. A lingering glance indicates that the communication channel is open. As you talk, hasty glances are used to obtain feedback concerning the person's reaction to what is being said.

The eyes, therefore, are used to convey emotions as well as to regulate conversations and obtain feedback. People of high status command much greater eye contact than people of low status. The manager who receives a great deal of eye contact from his employees can assume that he is perceived as a high-status individual.

FEET

From the eyes to the feet may seem like quite a leap but consider this scenario. Two men are seated facing one another. Mr. A is leaning slightly forward, his hands on his knees, his feet planted firmly apart, toes pointing outward. Mr. B, by comparison, is sitting well back in his chair, ankles crossed and tucked far back under his chair. Who is in command of the discussion, Mr. A or Mr. B? Obviously Mr. A.

Most of the time in the organization we can hide our feet behind our desk so they don't give us away. When an intense discussion is taking place, the executive who had been relaxed with one leg crossed over the other will assume the power position of feet apart, pointed outward. The opponent then can either assume the same position or indicate indifference by crossing his legs and leaning back in his chair.

Other ways our feet give us away are the "vine" of crossing one leg over another and tucking the foot behind the leg. This, of course, communicates timidity or lack of confidence. A swinging foot indicates impatience or nervousness while a foot housed in a dirty shoe is considered a sign of weakness.

VOICE

It is not enough to choose our words carefully and mask our facial expressions since how we say the words can in itself communicate. By changing word emphasis, a single sentence can be given many meanings. *Newsweek* described how Robert J. McCloskey, a State Department official in the Nixon administration, was able to use word emphasis to express the government's position. He had three distinct ways of saying "I would not speculate." Spoken without accent it meant the department didn't know for sure. However, emphasis on the "I" meant that he wouldn't but the questioner may—and with some assurance. Finally, emphasis on the word "speculate" meant that the questioner's premise was probably wrong. How something is said can be as important as what is said. Experiments indicate that when the vocal factors contradict the verbal message, the vocal factors are believed.

In this country a low voice is associated with positive personality characteristics whereas a high voice pitch is regarded as an undesirable trait, particularly for a man. Since everyone's voice has a range over which it can function comfortably, one's image is enhanced by speaking in the lower half of his normal range.

Another undesirable voice characteristic is the use of such speech disturbances as "ah," "eh," "uhm," and "uh." Goldhaber found that anxiety is reflected by long and frequent periods of silence. The more intense the anxiety, the more hesitant the speech becomes.

Psychologist Albert Mehrabian concludes that when someone talks to a partner whose status is higher than his own, the more the high-status person nods his head the longer the speaker's utterances become. If the high-status person changes his own customary speech pattern toward longer or shorter utterances, the lower-status person will change his own speech in the same direction. Mehrabian advises if you have an employee who makes you uneasy and seems not to respect you, watch him the next time you talk to him—perhaps he is not following the traditional low-status pattern.

POSTURE

Two men are talking. One is standing with his coat pulled back, hands on his hips, feet apart. The other is standing with his weight on his back foot, his hip thrown out, hands in his pockets, head down. Without hearing any of the words spoken it is probably accurate to conclude that the man with his hands on his hips is the superior of the man with his hands in his pockets. Probably one, if not both, of the men is angry.

Posture can often indicate certain attitudes. Rigid posture among men, for example, may signal dislike whereas relaxed posture among women tends to signal dislike. When several people are sitting in a group, the individual who stands or sits like someone around him may be demonstrating a desire to identify with them. In a conversation the more a person leans toward the person he is addressing, the more positively he probably feels about him. Along the same line, a person will tend to lean into the center of a group if he is interested in what is happening, and he will lean away if he is not.

An astute observer of a small group discussion may be able to predict who is about to speak by observing the changes of posture. Most people have one posture for listening and another for speaking. A change in posture usually begins with the person sitting up straight as if to prepare himself for what he is to say and the reaction it may produce.

THE USE OF NONVERBAL COMMUNICATION IN THE ORGANIZATION

Indications are that the successful administrator is more sensitive to nonverbal communication than his less successful counterpart. This sensitivity to the "silent language" can be learned.

Each of us has seen individuals who were promoted again and again over someone who was equally qualified. Perhaps personal variables were at work, such as "he creates a good image," "he makes a good impression," and "he has a warm personality." These perceptions are largely drawn from nonverbal communication.

S. E. Asch demonstrated that certain key labels can change the entire impression of the person. For example he found that such adjectives as "warm" and "cold" produced a widespread change in the entire impression. The "warm" person was credited with being more social, popular, informal, humorous, and better natured than the "cold" person. The manager who is described as "warm" thus has a significant advantage over one described as "cold."

Nonverbal communication in the organization is abundant. The individual who can understand it has a decided advantage over one who cannot. Whether you intentionally use nonverbal messages or interpret them, the end result is more effective communication.

WHAT DO YOU MEAN
I DON'T LISTEN?

If you have your ear to the ground, you cannot have your head in clouds.

Antony Jay, *Management and Machiavelli*

There has recently been an awakening concerning the importance of effective listening and indeed there should be. The busy manager spends from 40 to 80 percent of every work day listening. The higher he rises in the management hierarchy, the greater that percentage becomes due to more meetings, as well as to interviewing, counseling, exchanging of information, and decision making. Too often the result is communication problems. Why?

Poor listening is perhaps one of the most serious barriers to the communication of ideas. While hearing is natural, listening must be learned. Listening is making sense out of what we hear, and people in general do not know how to listen. Business communication depends more on the spoken word than it does on the written word, and the effectiveness of the spoken word hinges not so much on how people talk as on how they listen. Consider these examples.

A manufacturer of heavy machinery received a customer's order by telephone. The order called for sixty machine parts weighing nearly 100 pounds each to be shipped to a firm 1,500 miles away. Several days later the buyer called the manufacturer and asked what was going on. The order had been for six not sixty! The customer concluded, "Arrange immediately to get the extra ones out of here. They're using up valuable floor space."

A salesman stopped in for a quick hamburger between appointments. The young woman at the counter asked, "Can I help you?" The man responded "Cheeseburger, french fries with ketchup, and coffee—black." The girl questioned, "Do you want cream and sugar with your coffee?"

The managers of a large East Coast industrial firm went to work on a Monday morning and found their plant surrounded by pickets. It was a complete surprise. Top management had no idea a strike was impending, but they later learned that the firm's director of labor relations had repeatedly warned a member of top management that a strike was possible and had recommended action to prevent it. The firm lost five days of valuable production before a settlement was reached.

Such instances could be multiplied almost without end. Since business is hung together by its communication system, at all levels, the effectiveness of the spoken word and how well it is understood take on an added importance. An administrator can use effective listening to control many of the activities under his jurisdiction. But how do you become a good listener?

Dr. Ralph G. Nichols spent several years testing the ability of people to understand and remember what they hear. At the University of Minnesota he examined the listening ability of several thousand students and of hundreds of business and professional people. The general conclusion was that immediately after the average person has listened to someone talk, he remembers only about half of what he has heard—no matter how carefully he thought he was listening.

What happens as time passes? Dr. Nichols found that two months after listening to a talk, the average listener will remember only about 25 percent of what was said. The startling conclusion is that after we have barely learned something, we tend to forget from one half to one third of it within eight hours—thus we frequently forget more in this short interval than we do in the next six months. Thus, the businessman who spends 40 to 80 percent of his day listening will forget half of what he hears before the day is over!

Fortunately, our listening can be improved. Dr. Nichols found that students who completed a listening-training course improved at least 25 percent in ability to understand the spoken word. Some improved as much as 40 percent. In working with adult evening classes composed mostly of business and professional people, sixty men and women nearly doubled their listening test scores after working together on this skill one night a week for seventeen weeks.

Business and industry, recognizing the seriousness of poor listening skills, have instituted training programs aimed at improved listening. Some of the country's largest corporations— American Telephone and Telegraph, General Motors, Ford, Western Electric, and others—have their own listening-training programs. At least thirty-four departments of the federal government have followed suit as well as every branch of the military services.

A Self-Evaluation Test of Listening

Are you a good listener? A brief self-evaluation is presented below. Indicate how characteristic the eight listening habits are of you by circling M for *many times*, S for *sometimes*, and N for *never*. Try to be as honest as you can.

M   S   N   1. I cannot listen when there are distractions such as noise or an activity going on nearby.

M   S   N   2. I listen carefully to complex material.

M   S   N   3. I pretend to listen when I'm not listening.

M   S   N   4. Since people can think about four times faster than people can talk, I use the extra time to ponder what is being said.

M   S   N   5. When listening to another person, I am often bothered by the person's delivery and physical appearance.

M   S   N   6. I try to listen primarily for ideas and concepts not facts and details.

M   S   N   7. If a subject is uninteresting, I quickly dismiss the person talking.

M   S   N   8. When the speaker uses emotion-laden words or brings up taboo subjects, I try harder to keep my emotions in check so I can still hear what the person is saying.

The odd numbered items represent bad listening habits and the even numbered good listening habits. Any odd numbered items marked M indicate a need for work on that specific habit as does any even numbered item marked N. A discussion of eight ways to improve your listening effectiveness based on this self-evaluation test will be given later. First, let's consider the nature of listening.

The Nature of Listening

Listening is more than the mere hearing of oral messages. It is a complicated process which requires energy, understanding, and awareness. Three aspects of listening are: attention, reception, and perception.

Each of us is constantly surrounded by stimuli in the environment, the pleasant odor of perfume, a ringing phone, an attractive person. There are so many stimuli that one cannot pay attention to them all. Thus, attention is a selective process whereby one entirely ignores some stimuli, gives partial attention to others, and devotes full attention to still others. The first step in improving one's listening ability is to develop an awareness of where one's attention is focused. What do you hear besides the person talking? A conversation in the outer office? A typewriter? The screech of tires outside?

Since attention is a selective process, we listen to some things which are said better than to other things. For example, Jim

Thompson feels he deserves a promotion. When Jim's supervisor discusses opportunities and advancement in the company, Jim is really listening. However, when the supervisor describes several men who work with Jim as having "outstanding potential," Jim tunes out. Why? Because we like to hear things that relate to us, conform with our view of the world, and satisfy our needs.

According to Lee Thayer, the self-concept is an important part of the system. An employee with a low self-concept may listen carefully, during performance appraisal, to his supervisor's positive remarks concerning his performance. This information makes him feel good and improves his self-concept. However, when the manager begins discussing his weaknesses, the subordinate may well tune out. The man will leave the performance appraisal remembering the good and by five o'clock be totally unable to repeat any of the information about his weaknesses. The result is that the employee continues to perform exactly as he did before his appraisal.

In much the same way we dismiss information which does not conform to our view of the world. The manager who refuses to believe a labor strike is coming, the executive who dismisses complaints by his employees are examples. The head of an engineering firm became convinced of the advantages of the "open office" concept and had all offices redesigned. Engineers who had been with the firm for years gradually began changing their work habits, arriving early or leaving late. The number resigning to join other firms jumped. Deadlines on projects were increasingly missed. Still the head clung to his "improved" office design. He dismissed these changes as having nothing whatsoever to do with the new office layout.

How much we listen thus depends on our attention, and attention is influenced by our values, self-concept, and needs. We pay more attention to someone we like, than to someone we don't like. We pay more attention to someone in power such as our boss, than someone who is our subordinate. We listen selectively and because we do, we often get in trouble.

Reception is another aspect of listening. It is the process of actually receiving those stimuli to which one exposes himself. Perhaps it is best viewed as a physical process. We receive aural stimuli only to the extent that we can hear them. Yet reception overlaps with attention; if one's attention is focused on the traffic passing outside, he will not be listening to a suggestion made by a subordinate.

The third aspect of listening is perception. This is the assignment of meaning to whatever stimuli are received. In order for two people to understand each other, they must share similar meaning of words, terms, and phrases. If you tell a friend you will arrive a little before six o'clock, you may mean 5:55 but the person to whom you are talking may expect you at 5:45. When one of your employees suggests the Greenburg order can be done "right away," does he mean it will be out today, started tomorrow, or scheduled next week?

People attach different meanings to words. The meanings we attach are based on all of our past experiences. In the same way, these experiences influence what we see and what we do not see. Selective perception means that we limit the quantity of stimuli to which we attach meaning. For example, students who listened to presidential candidates were able to recall "acceptable" comments from the candidate of their preferred party, and they recalled unfavorable comments made by the other candidate. They listened selectively and thus remembered statements which agreed with their opinions and dismissed those statements which contradicted their view of reality.

Often these differences in perception show up when there is a difference in people's position. In one study of foremen and workers, it was reported that 76 percent of the foremen "always or almost always" elicited ideas from subordinates in seeking solutions to job problems. Only 16 percent of the workers, however, felt that they had been so contacted.

Barriers to Effective Listening

Due to the nature of the listening process—attention, reception, perception—there are many barriers to effective listening. Many of these are related to perception or the assignment of meanings.

1. We listen according to our own frame of reference, attitudes, and beliefs.

We each have our own window to the world. This window, built from all our past experiences, affects our listening process. Brent was twenty-eight and had worked for a research and development firm for five years. His work was considered satisfactory by Mr. Weicker, his superior, who generally considered Brent a good, solid worker. When business began to fall off, Brent became uneasy, fearing he might lose his job. After reviewing some of Brent's completed work, Mr. Weicker said, "You did a good job on this. It's too bad we don't have more projects like this one." Brent responded, "I know business is off some." Mr. Weicker glumly agreed, "It sure is." That evening Brent told his wife that he had to start looking for another job. When she asked, "Why?" Brent explained that Mr. Weicker had implied he should do so. "I'm not going to sit on my hands and get laid off like happened five years ago," he concluded.

What did Mr. Weicker mean? That Brent should look for another job? That large projects like Brent had been on were more satisfactory than the smaller jobs the firm was getting? That projects of that particular type were easier to manage? That the work to be done on that project matched the qualifications of the firm's employees better than other projects? Since the conversation ended where it did we will never know. Brent left convinced that he had understood exactly what Mr. Weicker had said. But did he?

2. We hear what we expect to hear.

If our past experiences with an individual indicate him to be sarcastic, we expect to hear him say something sarcastic. For example, a draftsman labors over his drawing plans and his superior comes by twice daily to look over his shoulder. The superior always indicates his dissatisfaction with a sarcastic remark. The draftsman works harder and strives to improve. One morning, his superior again approaches him, inspects his work and says simply, "Good job."

The draftsman explodes, "It's the best I can do! You want me to quit, well okay." The superior, surprised by the outburst, watches as the man begins to pack his things. In frustration he turns to another draftsman and says, "All I said was 'Good job.' " Since past experience indicated to the draftsman that his superior was sarcastic, he had interpreted this remark as further criticism.

3. We listen better to some people than others.

A person's position or power influences how well we listen to them. The subordinate will give close attention to a supervisor's comments, but the supervisor will not listen as closely to a subordinate's suggestion. If the person who is speaking to us has power, authority, or prestige, we listen closely and give much effort to interpreting communication from that individual.

These three barriers to effective listening result from the nature of the listening process: attention, reception, and perception. Since perception, the assignment of meanings to words, varies with each individual, communication breakdown can occur. By being aware of the role that perception plays in our listening, we are able to become more accurate in our listening.

WHY IS LISTENING SO DIFFICULT?

You are at an important executive meeting to make final decisions on next year's fiscal budget. The accountant is presenting his detailed report, some of which you have already heard. You suddenly realize you have been thinking about a decision that must be made when you get back to your desk. You are jolted back to reality and wonder how much you have missed. Did your attention wander for a few seconds, two minutes, five minutes?

We have all experienced the inability to concentrate. When we listen, the problem becomes more acute. Basically, this problem is caused by the fact that we think much faster than we talk. The average rate of speech for most Americans is around 125 words per minute. Compared with its capabilities, the brain processes words at a very slow rate.

When we listen, therefore, we continue thinking at a high speed while the spoken words arrive at a slow speed. While we listen, we still have some spare time to think. The use or misuse of this spare thinking time holds the answer to how well a person can concentrate on the spoken word. Thus, in order to listen better we must learn to use this spare thinking time efficiently.

EIGHT WAYS TO IMPROVE YOUR LISTENING

Listening is a difficult and complex process, but there are eight ways to improve your listening effectiveness. These will be presented in the same order as the items on the self-evaluation test. Thus, if you missed item 4 on the self-evaluation test, you may particularly be interested in number 4 below.

1. Resist distractions. A good listener constantly fights distractions. We live in a noisy environment but many distractions can be avoided—hold all phone calls, shut the door, move closer to the speaker. If the distraction persists, the listener must concentrate as intently as possible. This may not be easy. At one large Midwestern university 82 percent of the students queried reported "inability to concentrate" as their central problem in school.

We are all attentive to something during all our waking hours. If we can develop an awareness of where our attention is, we can redirect it from the distraction and improve our listening. Distractions are not only what we hear, but also what we see. In offices which have a conference room enclosed on three sides by glass, the poor listener sits where he can see activity outside whereas the good listener finds it aids his concentration to sit facing the solid wall. This is one way of avoiding distractions.

2. Exercise your mind. Many people avoid difficult—tough, technical, expository—material. The poor listener prefers material that is light, amusing, and easy. Whenever he is faced with listening to a complex explanation, and increasingly we all are, he cannot deal with it. To be able to listen effectively to complex material, the listener must practice. Effective listeners seem to go out of their way to expose themselves to unfamiliar subject areas.

Incidents created by poor listening to complex material have resulted in more and more communication being put in writing. Particularly is this true in business where it sometimes seems that every detail is recorded in a memo. This results in overflowing of written communications as few people have the courage to throw away a written "record." Perhaps the greatest loss from this new emphasis is the give-and-take feature of oral communication. If the listener does not understand a message when he hears it, he has the opportunity to straighten matters out then and there.

3. Work at listening. Man has always assumed that since he learned communication naturally as a child, it must be a simple process. That just is not the case. Listening is hard work and requires increased energy—your heart speeds up, your blood circulates faster, your body temperature goes up. Listen actively. The business leader must listen in many different ways so that he understands what the communicator says, implies, insinuates, desires, and hopes. The successful listener tries to understand facts, feelings, fancy.

For years high-pressure salesmanship was believed to be the mark of a successful salesman. All training efforts were aimed at the talking side of salesmanship. Many believed that glibness was magic. Today's salesman is likely to consider effective listening his most important skill. How he talks has given way to what he says. By working at listening, the salesman has learned to use on-the-spot information provided by the customer to determine how to persuade the customer to buy. For people who were always talking-oriented, the salespeople certainly had to learn to work at their listening.

4. Learn to use thought speed. If speech could be produced articulately and normally at 400 or 500 words per minute, many of our listening problems would disappear. Unfortunately, the average person speaks only about 125 words a minute. Since most people think at a rate equivalent to 400 words per minute, a gap develops. The poor listener uses this time to think about other things. His thoughts dart back and forth between what the speaker is saying and his own private thoughts. The good listener, however, constantly mulls over what is being said. By summarizing what is being said, he tests his understanding.

Rapid listening has been suggested as a means of avoiding this thought speed gap. A whole new technology of "compressed speech" is being developed and has been tried at a number of professional meetings. Major concurrent sessions at these conventions were recorded, "compressed," and played back at "listening posts." Interested people could then hear the sessions at a fraction of the time required in the original delivery.

The days of technology altering our listening habits are still some time away so the good listener must try to discipline himself and use thought speed productively. How? Research indicates that good listeners regularly engage in four mental activities, each geared to the oral discourse and taking place concurrently with that oral discourse. Again Dr. Nichols, a listening expert, concludes that all four of these mental activities are neatly coordinated when listening works at its best. They tend to direct a maximum amount of thought to the message being received, leaving a minimum amount of time for mental excursions or sidetracks leading away from the talker's thought. The four processes are:

1. The listener tries to anticipate what a person is going to talk about and what conclusions will be drawn.
2. The listener weighs the evidence the speaker uses to make his points.
3. The listener periodically reviews and summarizes what has been said.
4. The listener tries to determine what meaning is conveyed but not put in spoken words.

Because of the difference in the speed we think and the rate at which people talk, there is time for the good listener to use these four processes, but they do require practice.

5. Focus on the speaker's meaning, not his delivery or appearance. The effective listener is able to disregard the speaker's clothes, hair style, voice characteristics, mannerisms, and record of past experiences with him. He focuses instead on finding out what the speaker knows.

Increasingly business leaders are emphasizing the importance of "upward communication." This emphasis increases the need for effective listening by management. The executive counselor for a large pharmaceutical firm concluded, "By far the most effective method by which executives can tap ideas of subordinates is sympathetic listening in the many day-to-day informal contacts within and outside the work place. . . . Nothing can equal an executive's willingness to hear."

Successful managers are those who listen to their employees as frequently as they instruct them. These managers ignore the way the employee talks and dresses. They ask themselves, "Does this man know something I need to know?" "Is he in a position to see things I am not able to see?" Effective listening habits avoid the terrific costs which frequently accompany poor listening habits.

6. Listen for the main ideas and concepts. The poor listener tends to remember facts and details whereas the good listener concentrates on the broader picture, the central ideas in messages. Every speaker gives cues to alert listeners to his important ideas. The effective listener recognizes these and thus understands the speaker's ideas. He remembers the facts only long enough to understand the ideas that are built on them.

Many people take a great deal of pride in "getting the facts," but often the listener actually catches a few facts, garbles others, and completely misses the remainder. Why? He is so busy trying to memorize the facts that he misses the broad areas of what is being said. For example, a supervisor begins, "Now you must remember this; it is very important!" The employee listens intently to Fact 1. While he is repeating Fact 1 to himself to insure he will remember it, the supervisor has proceeded to Fact 2. Quickly the employee tries to catch up, but while he is memorizing Fact 2, the supervisor is on Fact 3. This process continues and the employee is hopelessly behind and has no chance at remembering the ideas or concepts the supervisor is presenting. The effective listener concentrates on grasping the ideas.

7. Actively seek areas of interest. Poor listeners tune out a conversation if the first few sentences are dull. The good listener always asks himself, "What is being said that I might use?" By staying with the conversation, the person may be able to find an element of value.

How motivated we are to listen depends on who is talking and what he is talking about. Obviously if our boss talks about deep sea fishing and we have no interest in it whatsoever, we will nevertheless listen intently. He is, after all, the boss. However, the good listener is one who is motivated to listen regardless of who the speaker is. From his viewpoint, if another person wishes to communicate with him, then whatever that individual says is important.

8. Be aware of emotional filters. Listening is affected by our emotions. Whenever someone touches our most private notions, prejudices, and biases, figuratively we reach up and mentally turn off what we do not want to hear. On the other hand, when someone says what we really want to hear, we listen openly and attentively.

What can we do about these emotional filters? Put simply, hear the man out. Withhold your evaluation even though it may require great self-control. The listener should try to comprehend each point made by the talker. Judgments and decisions should be reserved until the talker has finished.

It is human nature to search for evidence which proves us right in what we believe, but try to search instead for negative evidence, that which proves us wrong. This is difficult to do but the gain may be great—a real breadth of outlook.

NONVERBAL LISTENING

Do you listen best when you are relaxed—hands clasped behind your head, feet propped on your desk? Some people believe they do, but what is their posture communicating to the speaker? Posture expresses a person's attitudes—his feelings for the people he's with. The person who listens with his feet propped on his desk

42

may be subtly communicating lack of respect for the speaker and what he has to say. Certainly when you listen to your superior you do not assume that posture.

We go through every day "reading" the nonverbal clues of those around us. Posture can be a tip-off as to whether two people like one another or not, and the signals are slightly different for men and for women. The good listener is busy "reading" nonverbal clues while he is listening to the spoken words.

If you are discussing a new product with a subordinate who lounges far back in his chair, what is his posture communicating? Probably that he doesn't like you. When a man is leaning forward slightly but is relaxed with his back a little curved, he probably likes the person he is with and is being a good listener. If the conversation is interpreted as threatening by the subordinate, he would sit straight and tense, probably both feet on the floor.

Women show their dislike by lounging back in the chair and their liking by the same easy, forward motion as the man. Women, however, sit at attention for nobody of either sex, and no woman is threatening enough to make any man sit tensely at attention. Thus, the perfect listening posture is leaning forward slightly with your back a little curved.

Another important nonverbal aspect of listening is the eyes. Our eyes regulate our conversation. During the everyday exchange of words, while people focus their attention on what is being said, their eye movements provide a system of conversational traffic signals, notifying another individual when it's his turn to talk.

Let's consider an example. Mr. Bradley enters the conference room and exchanges preliminary greetings with an employee who once worked in his division. To indicate his friendliness he asks the man how he has been. The employee, Mr. Lambert, begins his response by looking away from Mr. Bradley. As he hits his conversational stride, he glances back at Mr. Bradley from time to time, usually as he pauses at the end of a phrase or sentence. If Mr. Bradley nods his head or murmurs "uh-huh" or otherwise indicates that he's listening, the employee looks away again and continues talking. When he finishes what he has to say, Mr. Lambert gives a significantly longer glance, indicating that it is the manager's turn to talk. When Mr. Bradley takes up the conversation, Mr. Lambert spends much more time looking at him than he did when he himself was the speaker. His away glances are generally few and brief. He makes reassuring signs when their eyes meet.

It's not too hard to see what is really happening here. When Mr. Lambert is speaking, he glances at Mr. Bradley from time to time for feedback: to make sure he's listening, to see how he's reacting, or for permission to go on talking. While Mr. Bradley is doing the talking, he looks at him quite a lot to show that he's paying attention, that he's polite.

In order to have a satisfactory conversation, you must observe these rules of eye movement. What happens when they are not? An individual can actually express many things by his eye behavior, just by exaggerating slightly the pattern. By looking away continually while listening, he indicates dissatisfaction with what the other person is saying. By looking away continually while speaking, he indicates that he is uncertain about what he's saying. To be effective the manager should look at the person while listening, thus indicating agreement or simple attention. The manager who looks at the person while speaking, indicates that he's interested in how the other is taking his remarks and that he's pretty sure of what he's saying.

When people want to hide some aspect of their inner feelings—fear, tension, anxiety, nervousness—they often try to avoid eye contact. The subordinate, for example, by asking a question but not looking at you is indicating his anxiety.

Another important nonverbal indicator is the hands. Gestures do communicate and at times they can unintentionally reveal emotions. Tightly clasped hands or hands that fidget are the most common clues to tension. By being aware of the speaker's nonverbal communication, you are in a better position to correctly interpret what he is saying.

Emphatic Listening

Emphatic listening occurs when the listener tries to perceive messages from the speaker's frame of reference. By contrast, deliberative listening views listening as an ability to hear information, analyze it, recall it at a later time, and draw conclusions from it. Charles M. Kelly distinguishes between emphatic and deliberative listening in this way: the deliberative listener first has the desire to critically analyze what a speaker has said, and secondarily tries to understand the speaker (this can be the result of personal inclination or of training which emphasized procedure at the expense of listening). The emphatic listener has the desire to understand the speaker first, and, as a result, tries to take the appropriate action.

In a discussion between manager and subordinate, emphatic listening can be useful. Not only does the manager need to know what the information is but why it is. For example, a black woman who has worked for the company for two years complains that no black women have been promoted in that time whereas three white women and four men have been. Deliberative listening would focus propriate response. Emphatic listening would consider that the woman has been a good worker for two years and needs assurances that the company will provide her with advancement opportunities. The manager would hear her saying, "What about me and other black women?" The deliberative listener might respond by restating the company's policy on equal employment opportunities, but the emphatic listener would respond in a more personal way.

Empathy is understanding and doesn't necessarily involve agreement. The manager might respond, "I understand what you are saying and you have some very good points—but I don't agree with them. Here are my reasons." By practicing emphatic listening, you listen without arguing or passing judgment on what is being said at the time. The listener can make his position clear later.

The emphatic listener tries to "hear between the lines." By listening he tries to hear what is not said as well as what is said. Take the case of Supervisor Henry. One of his employees, David, reports, "Well, it's done. I finally finished the Beck Co. order. It went out right on time. Everything is upside down but it's out. These emergency jobs sure cause havoc. My people are really ready for Friday and so am I."

The supervisor responds, "Fine. I have got the new schedule ready. We'll start with where we left off on the Martin job."

Obviously Supervisor Henry could not care less how David and his workers feel about emergency jobs. There are a number of things David may have been trying to say—I hate emergency jobs, they upset me, they upset my workers, I'm exhausted and so are they, how about a compliment for getting a hard job done on time? We cannot know exactly what because Supervisor Henry was not an emphatic listener. The sensitive manager will hear what the other person is inhibited from stating directly due to position held, emotions, or whatever.

The emphatic listener often uses the phrase, "What I hear you saying is . . . ." A manager listens to a subordinate outline a problem on a highly important project. The manager responds, "What I hear you saying is . . ." and restates what he heard. This feedback enables the manager to check or validate his impressions. One study showed that workers understand less than 25 percent of what their managers thought they understood. By using feedback the misunderstandings between various organizational levels can be minimized.

Feedback is time-consuming but it is well worth the effort. Only when messages are effectively sent and received can communication problems be lessened.

Listening to a Superior

Philip and William Anthony have identified three difficulties which may occur when a subordinate listens to you. He might resent interference in an area for which he feels responsible. He might welcome the suggestions or commands, but not fully understand them. He might fully understand the recommended course of action, but disagree with it.

If the subordinate views your message as interference, he is likely to interpret your suggestions as a personal criticism of him and his performance. So the manager must try to modify his message to reduce this interference interpretation.

If the communication is not fully understood, the subordinate should repeat in his own words what he thinks he has been told: "What I hear you saying is. . . ." If the manager wants to insure his message has been understood he can suggest: "Tell me in your own words what we have agreed to do." This feedback is a means of validating the message. Subordinates should always be encouraged to ask questions.

The third situation, full understanding but disagreement, requires great communication skill. Disagreements cause tension, yet without a climate in which disagreements are allowed, a meeting of the minds is difficult, if not impossible. An effective manager has the courage to give subordinates opportunities to express their opinions and to discuss differences.

Listening in Progress Interviews

A manager or supervisor should spend half of a progress interview listening. What you hear depends on what you ask. Try to get meaningful information from the employee by asking questions such as: "What do you like most about your work?" "Can you suggest any improvements?" "How does this compare with other places you have worked?" "What phase of your work do you find most difficult?" Then relax and listen. This is a good time to practice emphatic listening.

The manager can use this opportunity to learn as directly as possible what his workers are talking and thinking about. For the worker the manager's listening may be an opportunity for him to "get things off his chest" and enjoy significant emotional relief. If a tirade is launched the manager need not elicit extra information but simply be willing to listen.

Group Meetings

The manager who conducts employee group meetings should spend most of the time listening to suggestions from the group. The

problem should be outlined and employees encouraged to participate in determining a solution. The manager should indicate he is
receptive to employees' comments and will attempt to understand
them.

At the meeting, the employee's listening might be enhanced if
he (1) informed himself ahead of time about the topic to be discussed; (2) made notes on the problem; (3) summarized the problem
and proposed solutions in his mind; and (4) listened critically by
evaluating the ideas and opinions with what he already knew.

THE ADVANTAGES OF EFFECTIVE LISTENING

Effective listening produces many worthwhile results:

1. It improves interpersonal relationships. The good listener
indicates that he is willing to understand and respect the speaker.
As the conversation continues the speaker appreciates the interest
shown him and reciprocal feelings of respect are built.

2. It makes other people better listeners. By your setting an
example of good listening, others try to repay the compliment
through more effective listening on their part.

3. It enables you to have the benefit of everyone's opinions and
ideas before you give your own. Making correct decisions demands
having as much information as possible. By listening effectively
you acquire as much information as the speaker.

4. It avoids misunderstandings and mistakes caused by inatten-
tiveness. The poor listener does not remember important information.

5. It helps you to understand your fellow workers. By listening
effectively, you will learn how he thinks, what he feels is important, and why he holds a particular opinion.

IMPLICATIONS FOR ALL OF US

Certainly bad listening is pervasive in organizational manage-
ments. The busy executive is bombarded with 2,000 aural messages
as he goes through a normal day. The messages are of all kinds:
informative, persuasive, and entertaining. Only one fourth or 500 of
the messages are received and assimilated.

Which messages are received and assimilated depends on us.
We listen with our own experience only, assigning our meanings to
the selected aural messages. When one director talks to another
director a 90 percent efficiency in transmitting messages may be
achieved. But vertical communication downward reveals an entirely different picture.

Pidgeon Savage Lewis Corporation of Minneapolis, an advertising and communication firm, made a study of 100 representative
industrial management levels. In these 100 industries there were

five levels of management above the workers at the bottom. At the top was a board of directors, followed by a presidential and vice presidential level, general supervisory level, plant manager, foreman, and workers.

The study showed that if the chairman of the board calls in a vice president and tells him something, on the average only 63 percent of the message is assimilated by the latter. If the vice president relays the same message to a general supervisor, 56 percent of it arrives. If the supervisor gives it to a plant manager, 40 percent arrives. If the plant manager passes it along to a foreman, 30 percent is received. And if the foreman gives it to the squad of workers who are his responsibility, only 20 percent of the original message will have passed down through five levels of authority to reach its ultimate receivers.

Can a good manager allow bad communications like these to continue? Obviously not. What can he do? As stated earlier he can listen. In a study by Loyola professors as to what are the attributes of a good manager, worker after worker who thought highly of his superiors said, "I like my boss. He *listens* to me. I can talk to him."

Listening can no longer be viewed as a passive function but rather one that demands your full energy, intelligence, and sensitivity. The results are well worth the effort. By listening to the people with whom we live and work, old barriers to communication are replaced by open pathways.

4

UP AND DOWN THE ORGANIZATIONAL CHART

It takes courage to accept reality, and resolution to find out what subordinates are really doing and thinking.

Robert N. McMurry

"I am the vice president of this company. I make the decisions and issue directives that put them into effect. My subordinates carry them out. That is the way that business has traditionally operated, and operated efficiently at that, I might add." So responded an executive of a large corporation when questioned about the importance of internal communication. Many executives share this authoritarian point of view, but increasingly administrators are coming to believe that the objectives of their organization can be more easily accomplished by upward as well as downward communication.

The most basic principle at work in considering intra-organizational communication is: If no one will listen, no one will talk. A consulting firm was hired by an organization to determine why morale was low. A junior executive questioned by the consultant described at length what was wrong with the organization. The consultant, impressed by the analysis, asked, "Why don't you tell this to your management?" "They will not listen to anyone but senior management," he replied. As a result the company had lost several of its talented junior executives who realized that they could not use their talents to improve their standing in the organization. Pointing out weaknesses was considered being "critical" and making suggestions was considered being "pushy."

An advocate of the importance of two-way communication in today's organization is former Chrysler Corporation President Lynn A. Townsend. Good communication achieves corporate objectives, builds better teamwork, and makes money. Additionally it can achieve better quality and safety records, increase production, and reduce waste and spoilage. Townsend considers effective internal communication as an essential tool of good management.

The priority given communication at Chrysler was evident with the establishment of "Operation Better Communication," a comprehensive internal communication effort involving oral, visual, and written communication channels, and continuing research measurement techniques. A Communication Department was established at Chrysler headquarters and approximately 25 plant-level Communication Coordinators were appointed. All of this came at a time when the corporation's sales and profit were at a very low level.

Good communications start at the top. The chief executive who cannot face reality will find that his subordinates do not try to expose him to it. If top management is isolated it is because the managers choose to be isolated. A general principle in two-way organizational communication is that subordinates "read" their bosses better than is usually realized and bosses "read" their subordinates less well than they think.

Effective communication within an organization makes not only happy employees but more productive ones as well. In one study 81 percent of the personnel said the company "tries to keep me informed" while 86 percent said the company "tries to give employees a fair deal." By contrast, in a plant where communication was considered to be poor, 34 percent of those interviewed said the company tried to keep them informed and 58 percent said the company tried to give "a fair deal."

Scott Myers points out the importance of communication and productivity by examples of two assembly lines. Paper carton factory workers were idled for a few hours while industrial engineers introduced improvements into their line. The operators clustered near the Coke machine, laughing, drinking Cokes, and smoking. When the engineers completed the installation, they briefed the operators on the changes and asked for questions. Receiving none, they assumed the installation completed. However, the new system proved less effective than the old system. The engineered changes had altered role relationships and the system failed.

A superintendent and foreman in an electronics assembly department involved the operators in planning and balancing their own assembly line and setting their first week's production goals. They achieved their Friday evening goal on Wednesday, and went on to almost double their final week's goal. From a technical point of view, the electronic assembly line was not as well designed as the paper carton line, but it worked, Myers concludes, because the operators made it work. It was their system, not someone else's, and they made it work.

For many years leaders of organizations have focused on the technical aspects necessary to meet their goals. The result has been a rather romantic notion that if the computer is big enough, the new machine fast enough, and the technician trained enough, all problems will vanish and profits will soar. We are now seeing a much needed reversal of this trend. People are seen as the solution as well as the problem. For today's executive, there are increasingly as many consultants trained in human relations as there are those trained in physical sciences. This rediscovery of the forgotten worker has brought with it a new emphasis on upward communication in the organization.

Since communication is dynamic, it must flow through all levels of an organization. For this to happen, management must establish policies which encourage the unrestricted flow of ideas, up, down, and horizontally. By so doing they are going a long way toward preventing explosive situations which can arise in any organization. Employees who have an opportunity to talk to management feel a part of their unit or company and tend to support the policies which they helped develop.

The executives of Johnson & Johnson and affiliated companies, using the syndicate system of learning, attacked the problem of upward communication. In their report they gave four reasons why upward communication is of value to superiors and four reasons why it is of value to subordinates.

The superiors benefit in these ways:

1. Upward communications tell us not only when our people are ready to hear our story, but also how well they accept our story when we do tell it. We have no better means than upward communication of knowing whether our downward communications have been believed.

2. If we are to gain understanding and full acceptance of our decisions, subordinates must be given the opportunity to participate in their making or at least to discuss the merits and defects of proposed actions.

3. From upward communication we discover whether subordinates get the meaning from downward communication that is intended by the superior.

The Johnson & Johnson report listed these three reasons why upward communication is of value to subordinates:

1. Upward communication helps satisfy basic human needs. We respect our employees' dignity only when we allow, or better still invite, them to express their reactions to what is told— preferably before action is taken.

2. Employees who are encouraged to talk directly and frankly with their superiors get a release of emotional tensions and pressures which otherwise may find outlet in criticism to other members of the company and the community, or in loss of interest or efficiency.

3. Industry in its organization is essentially authoritarian which makes it even more necessary that every opportunity be given subordinates to express their views freely and to make their influence felt.

Even if there is an agreed-on need for upward communication, achieving it is nevertheless difficult. The very nature of an organization, composed of different levels and status, inhibits the free flow of information. There are many barriers to upward communication.

BARRIERS TO UPWARD COMMUNICATION

Probably the greatest constraint on upward communication is the filter effect, the withholding of communicating information which is potentially threatening or detrimental to the superior or subordinate. This involves the withholding of bad news, unfavorable opinions, and reports of mistakes or failures. Many subordinates fear reprisal in the form of promotions or salary increases being denied. The result is what information is conveyed upward often is slanted to make the sender look as good as possible. This filter effect may mean that important information is not forwarded up the organization to top management.

Another obstacle to upward communication is an unfavorable climate established by the chief executive of the organization. In a small public organization of fifteen employees the director always emphasized that he was open to communication. He believed himself to be a "modern" manager who utilized his manpower effectively. However, the new staff members quickly realized that this was all a game that he talked. In reality he ran an extremely authoritarian office and the result was a turnover rate of 30 percent a year. The director would assign his staff tasks and then systematically reject what the staff member had done. To replace all of the parts he found unacceptable he would then make his suggestions which, of course, the staff member would find agreeable.

The result was a massive game which the staff soon labeled "bloodletting." The staff member would spend days preparing an elaborate presentation which would be rejected and replaced with what the director had wanted all along. He would do this in the name of free and open communication with his staff. Needless to say, he was depriving his staff members of their feelings of worth and dignity and their only option was to resign, which they frequently did.

Another barrier to upward communication is the tendency to regard criticism by employees as a healthy blowing off of steam which can be ignored. Employees know when they are being ignored, and it does not take them long to see a pattern to management's reaction to their complaints.

Many organizations have no formalized mechanism for getting employees' reactions, questions, and ideas. Since the employees have no means to convey their opinions, they feel stymied and frustrated. A not-for-profit organization of about 2,000 employees had a number of divisions that were being operated in the red. The top administrators decided that a reorganization was needed. For six months the employees, mostly research scientists, arrived at work wondering if today would be the day the big announcement would be made. The employees with least seniority worried that they would be fired, and many actively sought other jobs. By doing so, they spread word of the organization's difficulties to others in the same field.

Finally the employees arrived at work one morning and saw a new division chief who later that morning issued a memo announcing his appointment. Of course, that new man was not able to pull the division out of the red. The people resented not being kept abreast of developments and the result was the division's problems actually increased. If a mechanism for getting employees' questions, ideas, and concerns had been available, much time and money would have been saved.

Another barrier to upward communication is poor listening at every level. Many subordinates take the attitude that the safest way is to say nothing. The superior's attitude and behavior in listening often either encourage or discourage communication. If the boss seems impatient, anxious, uncomfortable, or distressed by what is being said, he will likely not hear it again. However, that does not mean that it no longer needs to be said. The problem remains and although "no news is good news" in this instance the news is in the silence.

Listening is time-consuming. Many executives feel they simply cannot afford the time that it takes for upward communication. However, listening in many cases is a time-saver. By listening to employees' present problems, future ones can be solved before they become too big.

Alfred Vogel reported the results of a study conducted by Opinion Research Corporation among employees and their immediate bosses on the climate for upward communications in industry. Included in the research were engineers and scientists, white collar employees, hourly employees, and their immediate supervisors in eight companies. The desire to be heard proved widespread among employees with about 90 percent saying it was "very" or "fairly" important to them to be able to discuss their ideas about work problems with higher management. The desire proved as strong in the production worker as in the engineer or clerical employee, and as strong among women as among men.

The survey showed that over half the employees studied complained of lack of opportunity to make contact with those above their immediate supervisor. One of every two concluded that expressing his true feeling about the company to his boss could be dangerous. Fear of retaliation by blocking promotions was widespread.

Of all employees surveyed, almost three of every four agreed that many problems important to an employee are not considered important by management. Vogel concludes that his studies show that employees do not give their supervisors high grades on various facets of the upward communications job. For example, typically only about one-third of the employees rate their boss as "good" on being easy to see with a problem and only about one-quarter rate him "good" on such matters as ability to handle complaints and encouraging suggestions.

Some supervisors admit to lack of skill and ask for more training in communications—particularly in how to listen, how to handle employee problems and complaints, and how to lead group discussions. More than 65 percent of all supervisors interviewed requested additional training in the above areas. When employees are asked to describe the things about their immediate supervisors that cause them the most trouble on the job, bad listening practices head the list by a long way.

Research on upward communication in organizations has identified the types of information transmitted and the factors that appear to have significant influence on upward communication. Katz and Kahn concluded information transmitted upward is about (1) the assigned job, performance, and problems; (2) fellow employees and their problems; (3) organizational practices and policies; and (4) tasks to be done and how to do them.

Five factors that appear to have significant influence on upward communication effectiveness have been described by Koehler and Huber:

1. Positive upward communication is more likely to be utilized by managerial decision makers than negative upward communication. Middle managers have a tendency to believe good news and pass it up the organization while discounting bad news.

2. Upward communication is more likely to be utilized by managerial decision makers if it is timely. Data that arrive when a decision is at hand are given more significance than those which arrived earlier.

3. Upward communication is more likely to be accepted if it supports current policy. Information which reinforces a policy is accepted while evidence of the policy not working may be ignored.

4. Upward communication is more likely to be effective if it goes directly to a receiver who can act on it. Messages which pass through several layers of an organization can become distorted or filtered before they reach the top.

5. Upward communication is more effective when it has "intuitive appeal" to the receiver. If messages from subordinates seem to reflect the "common sense" perceptions of their superiors, they are more readily accepted.

Every organization has a number of "gatekeepers" who determine what information is to gain admission into the communication system. After gaining entrance to the system, the information is shaped, modified, and changed as it moves through the channels of the organization. At each level the message is structured to strengthen that person's position and weaken the position of his intraorganizational competitor. Some use it as a weapon while others use it as a defense.

How then does accurate communication ever take place? Cyert and March argue that the biasing of transmitted information is corrected for by the counterbiasing of received information. Downs argues that every general was once a lieutenant and remembers the type of distortion he used when he forwarded information to his own superior. This counterbiasing is almost applied automatically by those who receive messages at every level of the organization.

METHODS OF UPWARD COMMUNICATION

While managers agree on the need for upward communication, it is not so clear as to how they hope to accomplish it. The "rank and file" become harder and harder to stay in touch with but so too are the individuals who occupy positions two or three levels below the chief executive. These individuals, sometimes referred to as the "executive rank and file," also like to be heard. A number of techniques have been developed for encouraging upward communication from these various levels of an organization, from the lowest to near the top. These twenty-five methods have been grouped into meetings, written, groups, informal, and other.

MEETINGS

The no agenda staff meeting provides an opportunity for members of the organization to say whatever is on their minds. Jere W. Thompson, president of Southland Corporation, holds a two-hour, no-agenda staff meeting every other Monday morning to which about fifteen people are invited. This type of meeting is also used by Richard B. Loynd, president of Eltra Corporation. Once a month he invites about fifteen members of the headquarters staff, from vice presidents to secretaries, to discuss problems and raise questions. The participants are rotated so that everybody gets a chance to attend at least a few times a year.

The "cracker-barrel" meeting has been used successfully by first-line supervisors with the people in their organization. Held regularly on company time, these meetings utilize the foreman as a means of passing information, ideas, problems, complaints, and questions up the line to management. At the same time information can be passed downward to the nonmanagement personnel.

Interviews held with past, present, and prospective employees can be used as a source of information. Every manager should meet with his subordinates on a periodic basis to hear their ideas and complaints. Additionally information from exit interviews should be compiled as many who leave the organization may be more truthful about their complaints than those who are still anxious to maintain their position and have hopes of advancement.

"Jobholders meetings" have proven successful for employees of Pitney Bowes, Inc., a mailing equipment and business machines manufacturer. Once a year the 4,000 employees meet with Fred T. Allen, chairman and chief executive of the organization, and other top company officials to sound off or seek information. Similar meetings are held for the 6,500 employees in the field. Questions can be asked from the floor or submitted anonymously in writing. It is company policy that all questions are answered, if not on the spot, then later by letter, company publication, or bulletin board. Mr. Allen is pleased with the results: "All this is paying off in excellent employee relations. Worker morale is high and absenteeism and turnover are below the industry average."

Some companies hold "employee annual meetings" which are conducted in a similar manner to the regular stockholders' meeting. After the company officials report to employees on the state of the company, questions are taken from the floor. Those organizations which have offices at different locations may hold a series of such meetings.

WRITTEN COMMUNICATIONS

Probably the most unusual use of a written communication is the one developed by W. Michael Blumenthal, former chairman of the Bendix Corporation and now U.S. Treasury Secretary. It is not what he does—writes a memorandum—but how he delivers it—hand carrying it to the lower-level executive himself. When he finds the recipient in his office, he usually invites himself in for a chat. He concludes, "It's a nice way to stay in touch."

One of the more traditional methods of upward communication is the suggestion box. That concept has been expanded and modernized by IBM. The "Speak Up Program" was designed to provide answers to complaints, comments, and questions. Employees were asked to indicate if they wanted the response mailed to their home or if they would prefer to discuss the problem with a qualified person. The results were that 90 percent of the letters received were signed and about 80 percent asked for interviews.

A committee of superiors evaluated the suggestions with two hundred to three hundred coming from every one thousand employees. One-tenth to more than one-half of all suggestions receive some reward.

Another method of responding to employees' questions is the question box. The purpose of the question box is to guarantee that the questioner can remain anonymous while also having his question answered. The response of management can be printed in the company publication or posted on the bulletin board.

The company magazine is also used as a method of upward communication. Letters to the editor can be encouraged and space can be provided for printing the answers to questions and explaining company policies.

Attitude and information surveys are an effective means of learning the general communication health of the organization. When top management is shown the results of surveys from their people showing morale to be a problem, it is hard for them to deny that the problem exists. Specific questions about the company can be asked and answered, but the survey is not a solution as much as it is a means of determining the parameters of the problems.

There can be no substitute for face-to-face contacts. In this regard administrators who have a large number of subordinates have found it helpful to use a checklist to keep track of who they have contacted. For example, at the end of the day, on mimeographed lists of their employees, they simply check off those people they have contacted. By reviewing the sheets, the superior knows who he has not seen for several days, weeks or months.

SPECIAL GROUPS

"Special councils" have been used by some organizations as a method of bringing employees and managers together to talk about their problems. These councils meet from two to six times a year and have a formal agenda submitted by both management and workers. The agenda is published and available to anyone interested in it as are the subsequent decisions on each of the items.

Nonmanagement task forces are another special group designed to help with upward communication. Frequently an attitude survey is taken to determine the issues that most concern the work force. After these are identified, a special group of nonmanagement people then attempts to resolve these issues. Everyone is notified of what problem is being studied, what proposals are made and what management's reaction to the proposals are.

Another special group that has proven effective for upward communication is the employee council. Every department or division in the company elects a representative to serve on the council. All employee representatives meet with management's representatives on a regular basis such as once a month. It is the responsibility of the employee representative to ask questions and make suggestions for his or her departmental members. It is the responsibility of management representatives to answer every question, if not on the spot, at the next meeting. The advantage of this type of meeting is that the questioner is protected because he or she remains anonymous.

A junior board of directors, composed of middle managers and others below that level, has been used by several organizations. Dan H. Fenn, Jr., and Daniel Yankelovich report that in one company that uses this plan 2,000 recommendations were made and of that number only six were turned down. The board makes policy recommendations and presents its arguments to the corporate board.

Every organization has a number of existing committees which can be used more effectively for upward communication. Issues which normally come before a committee such as one on safety, for example, can be liberally interpreted so that any number of complaints can be handled by operating committees. Since these committees have been in operation for some time, the members may work together much better and thus be more successful in dealing with an issue.

A grievance panel can also be used in this way. Since grievances are usually concerned with a large number of issues— promotions, workload, working conditions, interpersonal relations —administrators can learn much by analyzing the grievances of their employees.

INFORMAL CHANNELS

Having lunch or dinner with subordinates is nothing new but increasingly executives, faced with overwhelming demands on their time, are using such occasions for talking with lower level executives. Blumenthal on his visits to the hundred or so cities in which Bendix operates makes certain to schedule lunches and dinners with divisional executives at all levels.

Any Saturday morning a Budd Company employee can find president James H. McNeal, Jr., in his office. Most of the time that he is there is spent talking with subordinates. The word is that anyone who wants to get the boss's attention can do so on Saturdays. McNeal finds that being dressed informally, on a day with no ringing phones, no secretaries, no appointments, often contributes to a free exchange. "It's just a more comfortable atmosphere for sitting and chatting, about company business or about something else," he concludes.

While the golf course has long been regarded as a haven for informally discussing business, the tennis courts have replaced it at Pfizer Corporation. Chairman Edmund T. Pratt, Jr., rented time on one of Manhattan's indoor tennis courts and invited company executives to use it during the reserved hours. The result was that the executives got some much needed exercise and the chairman learned a considerable amount of helpful information before and after the match.

An executive's bar and lounge is another place to have top people meet informally. Southland Corporation opened one on the top floor of the company's Dallas headquarters building. President Jere W. Thompson says, "It's great." The lounge is open to about forty company executives and Thompson says, "The lounge helps us to get to know our people individually."

Supervisors' clubs have proven useful as a method of upward communication for middle and lower supervisors. Although mainly educational and social in nature, the clubs bring together many superiors from different divisions and encourage the exchange of ideas and opinions.

Several executives have found it useful to schedule a couple of hours a week for lunch in the company cafeteria. Robert T. Quittmeyer, president of Amstar, sits down with any group of employees, regardless of their level, whose table has an empty chair.

OTHER

Some companies have made use of the telephone as a way to communicate with employees and hear from employees. In some organizations company officials are available on certain days for an hour or two to answer questions. Technology has provided other interesting techniques.

General Mills has a program called FactFone which uses three units of a machine called Code-a-phone. This unit answers callers automatically, transmits a prerecorded message and records messages in return. The service is available to 2,900 employees of General Mills, many executives or professional people, in the Minneapolis area. It acts as a twenty-four-hour open channel for feedback from employees.

FactFone receives between 160 and 175 calls daily, and has had as many as 866 calls in a single weekend. Any questions are forwarded to the company executive who is best able to answer them and the answer is made a part of a subsequent announcement.

Another method of providing upward communication is the use of ombudsmen, readily available to all employees. Again employees can make suggestions or criticisms with a guarantee of anonymity. This system works only when the ombudsman has the attention of top management.

All of these methods of upward communication are aimed at providing the means for subordinates, whether vice presidents or janitors, to make their ideas, opinions, criticisms, and questions known to the top administrator or administrators. Every person, regardless of his position, must know that his worth as an individual is recognized. Only then will he feel a part of the organization and be interested in its goals and objectives.

Downward Communication

In order for that employee to be effective, motivation is not enough. He must also know what is expected of him. Norman Sigband divides the employee's need to know into two areas. The first is the job itself. He includes the employee's interest in what his task is, how it is to be performed, how it interrelates with other tasks to achieve the company's goals, where and when it is to be performed. What are his duties and what freedom he has within those limits are also considered.

Sigband's second area concerns the employee's relationship with his company, his community, and his family. Included here are such things as how much insurance his company carries for him, why the company's stock dividends are going down, what management thinks about the union's demands, and how management reacts to equal employment laws.

Downward communication thus is an important aspect of the internal communication of any organization. Surveys indicate that employees do want to hear management's side of an issue. Only with two-way communication can employees know what is happening and, just as important, why it is happening.

Five Elements in Downward Communication

Katz and Kahn have distinguished five different elements in downward communication.

1. Job instruction. What you are to do and how you are to do it best summarize this type of downward communication. Of course, some jobs require more instruction than others.

2. Rationale. This explains why you are to do it. That is, how

the activity fits into the overall objectives of the organization. Some organizations think this downward element is more important than do other organizations.

3. Information. This communication is related to the practices and regulations of the organization. Typically it is the kind of information found in the employee's handbook.

4. Feedback. Information about how well the job is being performed is feedback. It may be in an interview with the immediate superior or perhaps in a warning or threat of dismissal.

5. Ideology. This could be considered an extension of rationale. However, it seeks to justify the organization's objectives and to convince the subordinate to enthusiastically support them.

Unlike upward communication which is characterized by a "filter effect" and thus a shrinking of the message, downward communication grows as it moves through the levels of the hierarchy. For example, the top executive may make a bare statement of a desired result but the message will soon be added to include the means for achieving that result. When it reaches the bottom, the message may have become a fully detailed plan.

Like upward communication, downward is difficult to achieve. It means getting the right information to the right person at the right time. Not only must one be sure that the message is understandable, but every effort must also be made to insure that it cannot be misunderstood. In today's massive and complex organizations, downward communication frequently goes to individuals with different value systems. This means designing the communications to the employee's goals.

METHODS OF DOWNWARD COMMUNICATION

Written communication is used more frequently than oral in downward communication. The following methods are examples of written methods.

1. The magazine is used by many, if not most, organizations. Whether a sophisticated, multicolor publication or a few mimeographed sheets stapled together, the house magazine has been a traditional method of downward communication. There has been a shift from pictures of sportsmen's prizes and favorite recipes to more substantive topics—a speech of the organization's president and developments in government affairs and regulations.

2. Another publication which has grown in popularity is the employee orientation manual. Its purpose is to set out clearly and concisely all details on the organization's policies and employee's fringe benefits. The increasingly complex areas of insurance, retirement, vacations, and profit-sharing, to name only a few, make a written description essential. This manual assures that the em-

ployee has the correct information needed to answer his questions whenever they arise.

3. Another successful method of downward communication is the letter which is sent directly to the employee's home. The letter conveys a personal touch. One of its major advantages is that it can be used for a number of purposes including welcoming, announcing, informing, explaining a large number of issues, policies, problems, and developments.

4. An annual report to employees has grown in popularity in recent years. After Brunswick Corporation issued its first report to employees, it received more than 500 inquiries from firms seeking additional information. Included in the second report from Brunswick was a special form asking employees to indicate their views on being kept informed about the company's activities and financial position. Some 90 percent indicated they would like to continue to receive the report annually.

5. An employee always pays attention to anything attached to his paycheck. The message printed on a small card or slip of paper can serve as a brief announcement but is used only occasionally for maximum effectiveness.

6. A bulletin is used to announce changes in policy or procedures. Bulletins are frequently used to communicate the change to managers and supervisors who tell their employees. The major advantage is that they insure the same information will reach all of the subordinates on a certain level. Official bulletins are often written on a special paper or have a certain distinguishing characteristic such as a stripe or headline.

7. Bulletin boards have proven effective as a method of downward communication. However, they must be kept up to date. The location and use of the bulletin board itself communicate the administrators' view of its importance. One located out of the way, cluttered with announcements that are outdated, tells the employees that communication is not a priority. Conversely, a large, well-lighted bulletin board divided by neatly lettered headings, and always maintained in clean, attractive condition will contribute to the communication climate of the organization.

8. Some of the least effective methods of downward communication, according to a survey conducted by Harold P. Zelko, are morale posters, pamphlets on special subjects, and reading racks. Some companies still believe that rack services are worth the expenditure because they keep employees informed while building good will.

That same survey found that two types of oral communication were considered the most effective means of downward communication. Several types of oral communication are described below.

1. Individual face-to-face communication is still considered the most effective by employees. Robert N. McMurry, professor of management at the Havard School of Business, states that to keep communication failures at a minimum, personal contacts are necessary between top management and low level nonmanagement personnel. He also points out that by permitting personal discussions between the two parties with a direct "feedback" from the workers, misunderstandings could be eliminated.

2. Small employee meetings were listed by employees as the second most effective means of downward communication. The emphasis is again on the personal impact of a meeting as opposed to a written communication. These meetings should be held on a regular basis and emphasize the frank and open exchange of ideas and opinions.

3. Interviews can be used for downward communication purposes. These regularly scheduled discussions can be an opportunity to communicate information downward and have the advantage of being on a one-to-one basis.

4. The public address system when used sparingly can be a means for making important announcements. The difficulties are that it is impersonal and that subordinates may not listen to the message.

In considering downward communication, the administrator must be concerned with what the message is, who it is going to, and when. Timing should not be overlooked as it is an important consideration. Some messages are more acceptable at one time than another. The message must also be appropriately designed for the skills of the receiver. In a large organization this consideration adds to the complexity of effective communication as the skills of the receiver of the message may vary considerably from management to the assembly line worker.

HORIZONTAL COMMUNICATIONS

For years the importance and extent of horizontal communication went unrecognized even though there is more of it than any other type. A study of a textile factory indicated that the lower the level in the hierarchy, the greater the proportion of horizontal communications. Another study found that as organization diversification and personal specialization increased, the volume of communication also increased in order to maintain coordination. The Hawthorne studies revealed that organization personnel, even at the lowest level, talk to each other and sometimes achieve levels of understanding and coordination that challenge the organization's formal authority.

Communication among peers is one type of horizontal communication. It is natural for people to communicate with others at their same level in the organization since they probably share many things in common. It is this communication that keeps the organization operating smoothly. Problems arise which require original, creative solutions. These are frequently developed through peer discussion. It has been suggested that the peer group should always be given some task-oriented communication. If they are not, their communication may become irrelevant or destructive to the functioning of the organization.

For example, Organization M has three professional employees on the same level. A new departmental director is appointed but cannot assume the position for three months. During that interval the department's assignments almost grind to a halt. The employees begin to discuss their anxieties about the new boss. This is soon extended to criticism about their superiors' lack of confidence in their executing work assignments without immediate supervision. By the time the new director is on the job, the staff has a bad morale problem, and one is already looking for another job. Their discontent was fed by countless conversations on how bad things were.

Another type of horizontal communication is between members of organizational subunits. If all messages were sent up to the superior and down to the appropriate department, the result would be chaos. The system would simply collapse from too many messages. There is a danger too, however, in short-circuiting the system. The superiors may not be sufficiently informed of decisions made between members of different subunits.

Departmental heads are often reluctant to provide information about their activities to others. The top administrator must recognize this and decide who is to be informed of what topics and how (the medium). The most traditional mediums are written reports and summaries, meetings, and conferences.

Often communication between subunits is characterized by conflict. The larger the organization, the greater the conflict between subunits may be. This is because the larger the number of subunits, the greater the diversity of the professionals' expertise. Each of these professionals sees different aspects of a problem.

In a research and development organization the researcher's goal was to get contractual research. This was viewed as the life blood of the organization. However, when the researcher sold a project, the contract had to go through the administration channels. Here everyone's purpose was not to let a bad contract through the system. Thus, at every level lawyers and accountants methodically checked for any conceivable way the contract could cause "trouble" or reflect badly on the organization. Whenever any of the hundreds of projects got "in trouble," this team would redouble its vigilance. The result was that a process, designed to take two weeks and help the researcher, actually took several months and sometimes killed projects on which the researcher had spent many, many days!

THE GRAPEVINE

Every organization has a grapevine. It may be big or little, an asset or liability, but it is always there and can be used by the alert administrator.

In his study of the Jason Company Keith Davis found that the grapevine is fast and can be highly selective. As evidence of these characteristics he cited: A certain manager had an addition to his family at the local hospital at eleven o'clock at night, and by two in the afternoon the next day 46 percent of the whole management group knew about the event. The local representative of the company which carried the employee group insurance contract planned a picnic for company executives. The Jason Company president decided to invite thirty-six executives, mostly from higher executive levels. The grapevine immediately went to work spreading the information, but it was carried to only two of the thirty-one executives not invited. The grapevine communicators thought the news was confidential, so they had told only those who they thought would be invited.

Information on the grapevine follows what has been called the cluster chain. Rather than person A telling person B who tells person C, one person tells three selected others. Perhaps one of them tells two others and one of these two tells one other. Thus, not every individual who receives the information tells it. The person who receives the information and tells others is called the liaison.

In addition to the cluster chain characteristic, the organizational grapevine spreads information immediately after it is known, transmits information about friends and work associates of the liaisons, and gives the secretary a key role as liaison. The grapevine is strongest in those organizations which have poor communication climates. It tends to flourish when employees get incomplete or ambiguous information, or when a remark is misinterpreted.

Of course, information which is repeated numerous times tends to become distorted. People begin to speculate about the "real" meaning and soon those speculations are passed on as facts.

What can the good manager or administrator do? Begin by listening to what's on the grapevine. If what you hear shocks you, your communication may be lacking. If the rumors are fairly accurate, almost complete, and generally reasonable, your messages may be getting through the system quite well. When a rumor needs to be denied, employees should be furnished complete and full details through people they trust. Rumors do not just "go away"; quite the contrary, employees tend to distort future happenings to conform to the rumor.

Every organization has communication difficulties, but some have greater problems than others. While a "perfect" communication system is impossible, emphasis on systematic procedures for upward, downward, and horizontal communication is definitely the starting point. A good communication climate is not an accessory but rather is basic to a good organizational climate.

5

WANTED: MEETINGS THAT PRODUCE RESULTS

Committees are groups that keep minutes and waste hours.

Unknown

Can more than 50 million Americans knowingly waste their time, day after day after day? That's how many it has been estimated attend the 11 million meetings held daily. If one were able to eliminate those meetings which were not productive, probably only a small percentage would remain. When businessmen are asked to comment on the meetings they attend, invariably responses include: "a waste of time," "disorganized and rambling," "dull," "too long," and "pointless."

Nevertheless each year the number of meetings in every kind of organization continues to grow. It is estimated that managers spend up to 50 percent of their time in meetings. The group meeting has indeed become an important part of today's management process. Why? Because research has demonstrated that frequently a group decision involving interaction and feedback among group members is better than the decision of an individual. In this age of complexity, individuals with various expertise are often formed into a problem-solving group. Why then does the committee process frequently fail?

GAMES COMMITTEE MEMBERS PLAY

Committee members are frequently busy playing games. A few of these are described below.

"*Pressure cooking.*" A weekly staff meeting was held by a middle-level manager. The stated purpose was to "keep everyone up-to-date" or, in other words, to share information. The communication of the meeting, however, revealed the true purpose: "Do you have any new contacts? Any prospects for new contracts? How many people have you contacted? How many follow-ups?" This information could have been submitted in a weekly report or given in a face-to-face meeting with the manager. However, the manager wanted his people to listen to what all the other staff members reported so that they would be properly "motivated." The real reason for the meeting was not to inform but to pressure.

"*Status climbing.*" It is an unwritten organizational rule that the higher one goes, the more meetings he has to attend. Midlevel administrators, realizing that the meeting is a status symbol, have adopted it for their own uses. By holding a staff meeting one can demonstrate that he has several subordinates whose time he can command. Additionally he communicates that he is on top of his staff because he requires staff members to report directly to him on a weekly basis. Since these meetings usually have no other purpose than to show up on the conference room schedule, they are usually dull and pointless.

"*Window dressing.*" These meetings are usually special and are called by a person in upper management. In pretense they are to inform the group members of a policy "under consideration." When the leader asks for comments, he is supportive of those favorable to his "suggested" policy while he aggressively attacks any negative comments. The group members quickly catch on and unanimously endorse the new policy.

The head of a division of state government was particularly skillful at this game. After the window-dressing meeting he would publicly announce the new policy, "crediting" those who attended the meeting with the policy and directing any subsequent implementation difficulties to them!

"*Ego-building.*" This game is particularly popular among the recently promoted. By having a staff meeting the new boss is able to indulge in whatever psychological gratifications he may need. Since he probably spent years sitting through meaningless meetings while his bosses engaged in "muscle-flexing," he is eager to indulge in some himself. This usually includes a demonstration of subtle threats, sarcasms, irrelevant references to his past experiences and concludes with a rousing "go get 'em!"

"*Flim-flamming.*" A large number of meetings are held for purposes of flim-flam. If a policy, for example, has been continuously opposed by Mr. A, a problem-solving committee is formed.

The committee is loaded with individuals who favor the particular policy Mr. A opposes. After extensive debate and argument, the chairman calls for the vote. Surprise, surprise, the policy is adopted. Mr. A as a member of the committee now feels he must support the committee's decision. After all, hadn't he been a member of the committee and hadn't the committee allowed him to make his argument as forcefully as he could?

"*Gang beating.*" Mr. X concluded the weekly staff meeting by telling Ms. Z that her presentation of the evaluation program was unacceptable. He suggested she rework her proposal and present it at the next meeting. Preceding that meeting Mr. X reminded several staff members of the upcoming presentation and suggested they give it a "thorough analysis." After Ms. Z made her presentation, staff members began to tear it apart. The torrent of criticism continued until Mr. X decided there had been enough and called for the next item on the agenda. Ms. Z soon began to look for another job, no doubt exactly what Mr. X had hoped.

"*Vacationing.*" Although participants may attend a meeting because of an interest in the agenda, some have their own hidden reasons. This is particularly true when the meeting is outside their own organization. Advisory committees of governmental or charitable organizations are sometimes composed of individuals who are either padding their community activities file or taking a few relaxing hours away from the rat-race atmosphere of their offices. Their main goal as a participant is to stay awake.

THE WHY OF GAMES

In order to understand why games are so often played by committee members, one must consider the function and purpose of meetings. On the simplest level a meeting defines the team, the group, or the unit. Everyone who is invited is "in," everyone excluded is "out." The meeting thus determines who the players are.

Additionally, the meeting provides an arena for the players. You have no doubt attended a meeting in which all players were obviously jockeying for position. This is particularly evident when a group is new. Everyone tries to determine their status in relation to the other members of the group. This behavior sometimes can dominate the proceedings of a committee but is not much in evidence in a long-established group that meets regularly.

In a staff meeting composed of persons who have a superior-subordinate relationship, there is one golden rule: the organization's system of reward and punishment is still operating. This system is based on the subordinate trying to guess what the manager thinks, wants, values. Most employees become good at this anticipation game, and those skills are used in meetings with just as much enthusiasm as elsewhere.

The committee member must frequently listen carefully to the communication of his (or her) fellow committee members and correctly interpret its underlying meanings. Writing in the *Harvard Business Review*, George M. Prince describes the communication at a business meeting where four men are working to improve one of their company's products—the familiar director's chair, which consists of a wooden frame and two slings.

Mr. First: Let's replace the canvas with nylon. (*This is an offer. It contains information and gives the contributor a feeling of worth and satisfaction.*)

Mr. Second: I think that's a good idea because it will give us better weathering characteristics. (*This is an acceptance. It gives approval to the suggestion and gives a reason why the idea merits approval. Both Mr. First and Mr. Second feel good. Also Mr. First views Mr. Second as a man of taste and an ally.*)

Mr. Third: Will nylon take the bright dyes that are used? (*This is a query. It is to be approached with caution. A friendly query only seeks information, but the unfriendly query constitutes a rejection. In order to determine which this is, Mr. First studies the words, tone, and nonverbal signals of Mr. Third. Participants in a dialogue often use questions to make an offerer either defend his contribution or see the folly of it. Perceiving the query to be friendly, Mr. First speculates comfortably and openly.*)

Mr. Fourth: That's a good idea, First, but nylon will stretch much more than canvas and the user will hit the supports. (*This is another kind of rejection. This is the ploy of appearing to accept but concluding with a rejection. Regardless of how nice a rejection is phrased, it is still a rejection and Mr. First will react accordingly.*)

There are thousands of ways to reject, according to Prince. By use of tone, an acceptance or query can be turned into a flat rejection: "Are you seriously suggesting we do that?" The same can be accomplished by a countersuggestion, silence, changing the subject, and other actions, many nonverbal.

In a meeting of several people, typically about half of the transactions are rejections. Although we are conditioned to accept rejections, we never are able to do so. Even mild rejection has a significant negative effect on people. Nonverbal signals are a decrease in the amount of facial expressions, crossed arms, or the head tilts slightly backward. The rejected person usually waits for an opportunity to even the score.

Prince continues the business meeting dialogue.

Mr. Fourth: I have an idea! We could double over this part of the fabric and—

Mr. First: That would increase our cost too much. (*The idea has been rejected before it was even developed. Too often this is how committee meetings go. The chairman, usually the superior, sees his role as shifting suggestions, pointing out flaws, and zeroing in on weaknesses. The subordinates interpret this communication as rejections. The result is that they try even harder to read what the boss wants or might find acceptable rather than trying to generate fresh, new ideas. A committee whose members are screening their suggestions based on whether they would be vulnerable if they submitted them, will be a poorly functioning committee!*)

Transcripts of committee meetings follow a familiar pattern. An idea is suggested and the other participants respond by pointing out all its flaws, shortcomings, and difficulties. Once the suggestion has been thoroughly worked over, it is discarded and the search is on for another idea.

The objective of the committee would be more quickly reached if members focused on improving the idea rather than destroying it. Modifications can often convert an unacceptable idea into an acceptable one. Frequently the reason this is not done is members are too busy playing their one-up games.

THE GOOD COMMITTEE MEETING

Planning is responsible for 75 percent of meeting success or lack of it. One of the most important aspects of planning is to decide precisely what you want to accomplish by means of the meeting. There will probably be one major objective plus secondary ones.

Every item on the agenda can be placed in what Anthony Jay, international management consultant, describes as four categories: (1) informative-digestive—this includes progress reports and review of completed projects; (2) constructive-originative—"What shall we do?" (3) executive responsibilities—"How shall we do it?" (4) legislative framework—this relates to the departmental or divisional organization, the system through which all activity takes place.

An agenda, properly drawn up, is an asset to any meeting. It should include some indication of the reason for each topic to be discussed. If one item is of special interest to the group, it can be mentioned in the cover letter or memo. Each item on the agenda can be described as "For information," "For discussion," or "For decision."

In placing the items on the agenda, the chairman should consider their implications. Those items which require creative thinking by the committee members should be placed first as the early part of a meeting tends to be more lively and creative. Items should be categorized by whether they are divisive or unifying. The atmosphere of a meeting is determined by the order in which these are introduced. Some leaders prefer to start with unity whereas others prefer the other way around. A unifying item is nearly always used to end the meeting. The most productive meetings are about an hour and a half; certainly little of value is achieved after two hours.

Whenever the committee meets to consider the agenda items, all communication falls into three categories: a message to get the group task accomplished (task); a statement to patch up some relationship among members (maintenance); or an effort to meet some personal need or goal without regard to the group's problems (self-orientation). A good committee meeting has an adequate balance of task and maintenance activities and a minimum amount of self-oriented communication.

THE CHAIRMAN'S ROLE

The chairman of a meeting has been referred to as its heart and will. It is a job which awards its holder prestige and glory in return for blood and sweat. Jay describes the ways in which an appointment as committee chairman affects different people. Some seize the opportunity to impose their will on the group and make incessant demands. Others are more like scoutmasters. The collective activity of the group offers sufficient satisfaction, with no need for achievement. And there is the insecure or lazy chairman who looks to the meeting for reassurance and support in his ineffectiveness and inactivity. Thus, he can spread his indecisiveness among the whole group.

What kind of chairman are you? A self-evaluation is given below. Answer each question as honestly as possible.

Y   N   1. If I have an idea on the topic under consideration, I always contribute it.

Y   N   2. I give everyone a chance to express his opinion, even if it seems of little value.

Y   N   3. If an idea seems too far-fetched, I dismiss it by calling for additional suggestions.

Y N 4. I summarize and relate the discussion to the purpose of the meeting.

Y N 5. I sometimes let committee members fight it out with each other.

Y N 6. I never let one individual, regardless of his position, dominate the discussion.

Y N 7. Chairing a meeting requires little effort.

Y N 8. I prefer to ask questions rather than make comments as they cause members to do more thinking.

Y N 9. I like loose meetings with limited agendas that allow members lots of interaction.

Y N 10. I let the members reach a decision all by themselves.

The good chairman would answer the even numbered questions "yes" and the odd numbered questions "no."

If the chairman is to make sure that the meeting achieves valuable objectives, he will be more effective as the servant of the group, not its master. A good leader severely limits his involvement in the decision. Many guard against making too many contributions by keeping count of how often they contribute and allowing themselves only a few.

One of the most interesting research findings in regard to group leadership is that there are two separate roles—task leader and social leader—which are performed by two different people. If the chairman chooses to be task leader, he tends to lose some of his popularity and to collect some dislikes. If he chooses to be social leader, he loses task leadership. Researchers found that at the end of the group's first meeting there is 1 chance in 2 that the task leader will be the most liked. At the end of the second meeting the chances are reduced to 1 in 4. At the end of the third they are 1 in 6, and at the end of the fourth they are only 1 in 7. Most chairmen prefer to keep the popularity rather than the task leadership. Both leaders are necessary to the harmony of the group. The task leader helps the group accomplish its work whereas the social leader assists with the maintenance and unity of the group.

As social leader, the chairman must deal with people problems. These can range from controlling the talkative to drawing out the silent. This can be done by picking a phrase from the talkative's dialogue, "Inevitable result, that's very interesting," and using it to draw out the silent, "Do you agree that would be the inevitable result, Murray?"

Another social problem is to create an atmosphere where junior staff members, in the presence of senior members, are not afraid to contribute. One way of doing this is to make a favorable comment about their suggestions. By making a written note of it, the point takes on added significance, and one can refer to it again later in the discussion. Another way of having all staff members contribute is to have the junior members make their contributions first. When someone of high authority suggests a plan of action, it is unlikely that anyone will oppose his idea. By beginning with the junior members, a broader spectrum of ideas will result.

The chairman should, of course, be on the alert for self-oriented statements. With senior staff members in attendance a junior may attack the suggestion of another junior in an effort to make himself look good to his superiors. An effective way of discouraging this is to require the attacker to produce a better suggestion. This communicates that you are not going to permit attacks on suggestions but rather constructive modifications leading to a workable solution.

The behavior of a good chairman can be summarized: listen to all members, and don't allow anyone to be attacked; have everyone contribute; severely limit your discussion; and keep things moving. How do you do it? By the communication you use. Much of it will be nonverbal.

As the chairman listens to group members he can try to hurry them by leaning forward and nodding briefly to show the point is understood without additional explanation. He can also indicate his indifference to the remark by rearranging his papers. Another sign of impatience is fixing his eyes on the speaker and tensing his muscles. On the other hand, he rewards the sort of contribution he is seeking by relaxing in his chair, displaying a look of pleasure and, in general, showing that there is plenty of time for the speaker to develop his point.

By using nonverbal methods in this way the chairman communicates to the group members what is expected of them. The meeting that is full of self-oriented behavior, rather than task-oriented, has the approval, probably nonverbal, of the chairman. Conversely, the highly productive meeting that begins and ends on time is accomplished partly by the prompting, verbal and nonverbal, of the chairman.

Active Participant or Passive Spectator?

The committee members can do much to insure the success of the meeting. It is important that they have a proper attitude toward the meeting. Mr. A was promoted to division director and had to attend weekly staff meetings. Since he had attended many poorly planned and run meetings, Mr. A did not believe the conference could be a useful tool of supervision and management. With this negative attitude he decided not to participate in the discussion. Finally one of his colleagues took him aside and pointed out the positive aspects: he could be benefiting from the knowledge and opinions of others; helping to formulate policy and decisions affecting his workers; and developing an understanding of the relationship between his division and the company as a whole. At the next meeting Mr. A had a different attitude, one of openmindedness.

The good committee member plans for the meeting by asking himself what its purpose is and how he can help accomplish that purpose. One's participation is only meaningful if he is totally prepared. This means reading any advance information received and studying the agenda. The member who thumbs through his materials underlining at random and putting large question marks in the margins will not really fool anyone.

By understanding how groups function, you will be a better participant. Particularly important is the timing of your remarks and their length. Studies have shown that if you participate early in a conference, you will establish yourself with the group. You will probably gain their respect so that they will welcome your future comments. However, if you wait a prolonged period before making a contribution, this tends to lead toward the group being less inclined to accept your comments. It also tends to keep you silent as a group member, for the longer you wait for your first comments, the more satisfied you become to remain silent. Remarks should be kept to about one minute in length or perhaps two minutes at most. This can be done if you talk a number of different times rather than trying to say all you have on your mind at one time.

Group Characteristics

There are a number of group characteristics which operate in any committee. An awareness of these can enhance the productivity of the chairman and participants. Included are size, cohesiveness, roles, conflict, groupthink, and risky shift.

Most consider the ideal group size to be four to six or seven with the most preferred number being five. This number is small enough for meaningful interaction, yet large enough to represent a range of inputs for problem solving and decision making.

Another group characteristic is cohesiveness. What is cohesiveness? It refers to how well the members like one another, how much friendliness is in the group, and the amount of desire to reach a common goal. Those groups with high cohesion have members who trust one another and are willing to give of themselves to the group. There are two levels of attraction: to the group members and to the group's function.

Of course, we have all attended committee meetings that lacked cohesiveness. Perhaps two individuals did not get along well. This conflict among members prevents cohesiveness. As a result the meeting was not a satisfactory one for the two individuals or the other members. Cliques are another barrier to group cohesiveness as they prevent members from functioning as a total group. The leader and participants should strive for cohesiveness as it will increase the productivity of the committee.

In order for the group to be cohesive, the members must be content with their status or role. The other group members determine the status to be accorded an individual, and by their actions indicate how much power and leadership he is to possess. You have probably been a member of a group which did not show you proper respect or recognize your actual worth. The perceptions of the members did not match yours. When this happens, the member is not pleased with his role in the group. By being a low status individual, less communication will be directed to him than those of higher status. Sometimes the status conferred by the group parallels one's title or position, whereas other groups may require that the status be achieved.

Conflict frequently develops not only within the group, but between groups and within the organization as a whole. Conflict within the group usually tears a group apart and decreases its accomplishments whereas conflict between groups brings members together and increases productivity. Some conflict is inevitable because members differ in their creativity, values, and needs. The conflict between groups can actually be healthy.

One plant actually lowered manufacturing costs by group conflict. During one afternoon the plant was shut down and employees were assigned to problem-identification groups and asked to list key problems facing the organization. At the end of the afternoon, each group reported its findings back to all other groups. Two weeks later the plant closed down again and a specific set of problems identified at the earlier meeting was assigned for solutions. For the next two months, the plant closed every Friday afternoon for the groups to work on their list of problems. The result was that costs and absenteeism dropped while morale and productivity increased.

Whereas intergroup conflict may increase a group's effectiveness, a group which is totally without interconflict may intensely pressure its members to conform. The result was labeled by Irving Janis as "groupthink." It often causes highly knowledgeable and experienced decision makers to make decisions that turn out badly. It has been suggested that the year-after-year continuation of the Viet Nam War was an extreme example of groupthink.

The committee suffering from groupthink never allows any criticism of the group's decision process or any of its members. The pleasant interaction of the group becomes all important and its accomplishments secondary. Since the cohesiveness of the group is high, any action, such as criticism or conflict, which would affect that cohesiveness is avoided.

How does groupthink come about? By the leader and participants indicating their unwillingness to consider ideas or suggestions which do not conform to their own thinking. Whenever the sales manager responds coolly or indifferently to the idea of a new salesman, it lessens the future introduction of new ideas. The members soon learn to limit their discussion to the acceptable topics and to express views which conform to the group's view of reality.

Another problem groups have is termed "risky shift." This is the tendency of groups to take riskier actions than individuals would do. This appears to be true regardless of the purpose of the group. Of course, this has significant implications for organizational decision-making committees. Findings indicate that the tendency to take risks increases under conditions of stress. Thus, a decision is made which is later repudiated by each individual member who insists he did not want it that way. The diffusion of responsibility represented by a committee often results in riskier decisions than if each person were totally responsible.

Nonverbal Communication in the Meeting

Only a minor part of the communication in a committee meeting is verbal—most is nonverbal. Emotions and feelings are projected in the same nonverbal way as they are elsewhere. Stress, for example, is shown by the person who tends to fidget, shift, or change his posture frequently. Edman and Friesen found that when a person feels uncertain about an issue, decision, or event, he resorts to a hand shrug whereas a person who is signaling an intent to answer a direct question tends to use a sort of open hand reach.

The body posture of committee members indicates their emotions too. When they feel knowledgeable and comfortable about a topic, their body movements tend to be frequent, vigorous, and enthusiastic. When the topic is unfamiliar or tension-provoking, body movements tend to be more inhibited or uptight. The story is told of a chairman of the board of a large corporation. He seemed to be inattentive and bored through most of the executives' reports. However, when the report began getting into a sensitive area, he would be alert and ready to pounce. The man claimed he knew when an executive had doubts because he could see it in his body movements.

A new member of a committee can tell a great deal about the group before the meeting even begins. A generally relaxed posture with much eye contact indicates a friendly, cohesive group. Conversely, when there is friction among members, postures will be tense, and members will be seen as leaning away from one another.

As the committee discussion proceeds, members use a system of nonverbal communication to help direct and control the flow of communication. Participants may use eye contact and a few quick nods to encourage the speaker to continue or discourage the speaker by not giving him any eye contact. Other nonverbal cues are eyebrow motions, shift of posture, and hand movement.

The flow of communication is also influenced by the seating arrangements. Where you choose to sit will determine if you are drawn into communication, how frequently you will speak, and what your role will be. Individuals prefer to sit across from others as opposed to sitting side by side. Those who tend to dominate the discussion tend to choose the more central seats—the end and middle seats at a rectangular table. These are referred to as the high-talking seats. The individuals who occupy them contribute and receive more communication than the other members. Tense, anxious individuals avoid these seats as they do not want to experience the increased eye contact and involvement that those positions involve.

An organization expanded its board of directors by six people. At the first meeting of the enlarged board, all the new members, except one, seated themselves in positions where they would have minimal eye contact. They spent the meeting looking interested, but without making any contributions. The other new member took the middle seat and got involved early in the discussion. At subsequent meetings he always took that seat, and in two years was in line for the rotating position of chairman.

New Discussion Techniques

As one examines how committees function, it becomes apparent that some individuals do not express their ideas, opinions, solutions, or questions. Several new discussion techniques have been developed in recent years to assist the overall group interaction. The committee's objective can only be achieved by the communication of members. Thus, each of these techniques is designed to stimulate communication. These new techniques are: nominal group procedure, brainstorming, buzz sessions, Phillips 66, posting, problem consensus, and RISK.

Richard Huseman suggests the nominal group procedure as a way to identify problems and generate solutions. When using this procedure, the participants assemble in groups but are told not to speak to each other. Each person writes down what he considers the advantages and disadvantages of the proposition under consideration. After each member has done this, a master list of advantages and disadvantages, without duplicity, is compiled. The next step is the ranking of the advantages and disadvantages on paper by each participant. This ranking establishes priorities.

The nominal group procedure provides balanced participation and stimulates ideas. Huseman concludes that there is no evaluation during the process and hence the climate is not threatening. Thus, the committee achieves greater productivity as well as providing more satisfaction to the participants.

Another discussion technique for developing ideas and facilitating their expression is brainstorming. There are four rules which must be followed: (1) Evaluation and criticism are forbidden. (2) All contributions are welcomed. (3) Quantity of ideas is desired. (4) Combination and improvement of ideas are sought.

Developed by Alex F. Osborn for producing new ideas, brainstorming was based on his observation that nothing has so inhibiting an effect on the production of ideas as concurrent criticism. Brainstorming provides a relaxed atmosphere and has the participants create new ideas which are written on a flip chart or chalkboard where all can see them. Participants must suspend their judgment and critical evaluation, focusing instead on their creativity.

Buzz groups is a technique which may be used to organize a large group meeting into many small groups which work concurrently. By dividing the audience into groups of four to ten, everyone has an opportunity to participate. A chairman is appointed for each group. The purpose may be to identify problems, to suggest solutions, to get questions for a speaker or panel, or to express views on the issue. At the end of the buzz group discussion, the chairman reports his group's opinions to the entire audience.

Another discussion technique similar to the buzz group is called Phillips 66, referring to the creator's name and six persons discussing for six minutes. The technique, however, can be used for secondary groups from three to eight with an appointed chairman. Phillips 66 is used to formulate questions dealing with an area of the discussion topic. When the discussion is completed, the questions are presented to the primary discussion group. This allows each individual an opportunity to participate. It is useful in pointing out problems and in raising important questions. The topic should be limited and require no longer than one hour of discussion.

In any meeting questions are often raised which are more premature or out of context. A technique for handling this is called posting, the listing of questions or ideas regarding the discussion topic. The chairman announces the time when posting will be conducted: prior to the discussion, during the discussion, or immediately following the discussion. All questions are recorded and if necessary ranked in order of importance. This helps the group to determine in what direction the discussion should go and contributes to group cohesiveness. The questions can be used to organize the discussion for increased productivity.

A modification of the "posting" technique is the problem census. John Brilhart concludes that it is useful for building an agenda for future problem-solving meetings, for program planning by an organization, or for discovering problems encountered by a group of employees that might not be known by a supervisor. For example, a group of salesmen for a feed company scattered over two states met with the sales manager to develop a list of problems and programs for a series of monthly meetings. The problem census technique requires the supervisor follow a series of distinct steps:

1. Explain the purpose of the technique which is to bring out all problems, concerns, questions, or difficulties any member of the group would like to have discussed.
2. Each participant presents one problem or question.
3. Each problem is "posted."
4. The group votes on the priority of each item on the list.
5. Each problem is dealt with in turn.

Another discussion technique, developed by Norman R. F. Maier, is the RISK technique. It is particularly useful in organizations as a way of testing reactions to proposed changes in policy or procedures before final decisions are made or to prepare employees for changes which are being imposed from above. The RISK technique is not used often but has been proven effective for smoothing the way to implementing a change in the organization.

The discussion leader must sincerely be interested in airing all possible fears, complaints, grievances, and problems as well as able to totally refrain from all evaluative or critical responses.

Maier outlines seven steps which must be followed: (1) Present in detail the proposed change. (2) Explain the purpose and procedures to be followed in the RISK technique, emphasizing that no criticism or evaluation is allowed. (3) Invite and post all risks, fears, problems, doubts, and concerns. Plenty of time must be allowed. Frequently the most significant items, those most threatening and disturbing to the members, do not come until late in the session. (4) After this initial meeting, the list should be reproduced and circulated to all participants. (5) At the next meeting add any further risks thought of in the interim. (6) Have the group decide if each risk is serious and substantive. (7) Risks which remain on the list become an agenda to be dealt with one at a time in problem-solving discussions with the solutions to be worked out by the group.

These new discussion techniques can be used to avoid many of the weaknesses of the traditional committee meeting. They provide for balanced participation, inhibiting the dominance of any one individual. By limiting and clarifying the group's objective, they increase the likelihood of achieving it.

EVALUATION OF EFFECTIVENESS

Having considered the effectiveness of thousands of committees which are meeting regularly, I think the old motto "practice makes perfect" should be revised to read "practice makes permanent." Bad habits have become a way of life and the committee plods along, carrying its burden like a turtle. The committee that is concerned with productivity and is results-oriented should be evaluated periodically. There are several strategies for evaluation.

One of these is the use of audio or video tape. It has been proven time and time again that members are so busy keeping up with what is happening as it happens, that they do not reflect on the interaction. By listening to a tape of the meeting, they find these interactions more apparent: Who is dominating the discussion? Is someone "shooting down" ideas as quickly as they are suggested? Were any questions left for later but never answered? Does the chairman interfere with the discussion? Impose his opinions on the group? By reviewing a tape of the meeting you can answer these questions.

Another way of evaluating a committee is to have an observer. Things always look different when you are sitting outside the discussion. A midlevel administrator conducted a meeting of citizens who supported a particular political issue. After the meeting, the administrator discussed how it had gone with two of his aides who had attended but not as participants. The views of the administrator and his aides were so divergent that it seemed they had not attended the same meeting! Why? Because the leader's attention had been on getting everyone to contribute to the discussion, to stay on the topic, and to achieve the meeting's objective. The aides had been watching the nonverbal communication of the participants. The result—the administrator concluded it was a good meeting while the aides concluded the participants were bored by the subject and length of the meeting.

There are two types of observers: the reminder-observer and the critic-observer. The reminder helps the group without offering any criticism. He comments on what the group is doing well and puts most remarks in the form of questions. The proper role is one of reminding, reporting, and raising questions. At the end of the meeting the chairman may ask the reminder-observer to report on his observations so that the committee can strive for improvement.

By contrast, the critic-observer is usually trained in group functions and makes a detailed report after the discussion. Included in it will be his opinion about the strong and weak points of the meeting. He may compliment the group, point out where it got off the subject, and criticize an individual's performance.

Whereas the observers are outside the group, Post-Meeting Reaction Sheets, or PMRs, are used to get objective reactions from discussants. Since these are submitted anonymously, a participant can report his evaluation honestly. The questionnaire is designed to elicit comments about the group and discussion. Examples are given below:

PMR
(Post-Meeting Reaction Sheet)

1. How pleased are you with the *results* of today's discussion?

very pleased	moderately pleased	not at all pleased

2. Were you pleased with the *leadership* of the chairman?

very pleased	moderately pleased	not at all pleased

3. Most participants' preparation for the meeting was

thorough	average	poor

4. What could be done to improve future meetings?

Another means of evaluating a group's effectiveness is the interaction diagram. This diagram, made by an observer, reveals who is talking to whom, how often each member participates orally, and any dominating persons. On an interaction diagram the names of all participants are located around the diagram in the same order in which they sat during the discussion. Each time a person speaks an arrow is drawn from his position toward the person to whom he addressed the remark. If he speaks to the entire group, a longer arrow points toward the center of the circle. Subsequent remarks in the same direction are indicated by short cross marks on the base of the arrow. This gives a visual display of the communication that took place during the meeting. Any pattern can be easily seen.

There are rating scales available for evaluating any aspect of the group and its discussion as well as for individual participation. These scales can be used by two observers who, working independently, rate the group and check the similarity of their ratings. Additionally, any number of scales are available for analyzing and appraising functional leadership.

Regardless of which method is used, it is important that the committee have some feedback about its discussion. This evaluation can be used to improve performance in future meetings.

Meetings can be one of management's most effective and productive devices—if the group dynamics are understood and a proper format developed. These meetings must be planned and not left to hope and chance. Dr. Norman B. Sigband, professor at the University of Southern California, emphasizes there must be: a need for a meeting; a friendly, cooperative climate; clearly established plans and objectives; preparation; and a competent discussion leader in charge. For the meeting that is held frequently, evaluations should also be made.

Meetings are here to stay but the boring, poorly run meeting need not be. With knowledge, training, and preparation, an administrator can make meetings one of an organization's best communication devices.

6

INTERVIEWING FOR FIRST-RATE INFORMATION

Good communication means devoting considerable attention to the information people receive in response to their own communication efforts.

Renato Tagiuri

Any administrator, regardless of his field, spends much of his time interviewing. Interviews are used for selecting, training, counseling, reprimanding, and even terminating employees. The purpose of the interview is to inform or persuade, and since we have been informing or persuading for so long, we often think we know all there is to know about the interview. By reviewing the basic principles of the interview process and the types of interviews, this book offers you an opportunity to make a systematic analysis of your own interview techniques.

An interview is the process whereby individuals, usually two, exchange information. Sounds simple, doesn't it? But this exchange often takes place in an atmosphere of urgency and sometimes tension. Interviews about grievances or reprimands frequently produce highly charged, sharp comments flying back and forth. In order to direct and guide the interview effectively, the manager must understand how to use questions.

OPEN VS. CLOSED QUESTIONS

The most important part of any interview is the questions. They determine the amount, quality, and kinds of information the interview produces. Questions generally fall into one of two classes: open or closed.

Open questions are broad, often specifying only the topic to be covered: "Tell me about your work experience." The respondent is allowed maximum freedom in determining the amount and kind of information to give. The interviewer can use open questions early in the interview as they are not threatening and easy to answer. An additional advantage of open questions is that they reveal what the respondent thinks is important—what he says and the order in which he says it. However, they do take a large amount of time and may produce information that is not useful for your purpose.

Closed questions are restrictive and limit options available to the interviewee: "What was your salary on your last job?" Such questions can be used for controlling the interview. They are generally used to get specific pieces of information. Of course, while you gain time, you may lose meaningful information since closed questions allow little chance for volunteering potentially valuable information.

USING QUESTIONS EFFECTIVELY

The interviewer can use a number of strategies to get additional information from the person being interviewed. Silence can be used to prod the person into continuing. If the person needs additional encouragement, the interviewer can rely on such phrases as: "Go on." "Tell me more." "And then?" Some successful interviewers simply use "Hmmm," or "Uh huh." For eliciting more detailed information, the interviewer might say: "Tell me more about . . . ." "Explain further about . . . ." "What did you do after . . . ?"

A reflective probe is a means of clarifying a vague or unclear answer. Examples are: "Then you think . . . ." "You mean by unsatisfactory that . . . ." If the interviewee has expressed a feeling or attitude that you want clarified, you might ask: "Why do you feel that way?" "How do you feel about that?" "Why do you think it is that way?"

The mirror or summary question can be used to check your understanding of what has been said. On receiving instructions from a superior, one often checks his understanding by saying, "Okay, let's see if I have this straight. I am to . . . ." This type of questioning can effectively be used in the interview to check your impressions. It is a means of eliciting direct feedback from the interviewee. For example, "Bill, are you telling me that the reason the new schedule isn't working is because . . . ?"

When one examines the question-answer process of interviews, two problems are the most common. These are irrelevant or inadequate answers from the person being interviewed and leading or loaded questions from the interviewer.

Since many interviews take place between people who have a superior-subordinate relationship, the subordinate may tend to avoid giving information which he believes might have an adverse effect on him. One way of protecting himself is to give an irrelevant answer. For example, Company X has had packaging problems. New materials were purchased and a new procedure developed. However, problems persisted.

Interviewer: Why do you think we still have packaging problems?
Interviewee: Well, you know how it is. A lot of people complain about changing the old way of doing things.
Interviewer: But the employees did not like the way we were doing it, and that's one reason we changed it. What do you think the problem is?
Interviewee: I think everyone is doing as good a job as he can right now. Maybe things will get better soon.

The interviewee is still avoiding the question. Either he does not have an opinion on what is causing the problem or he is determined not to tell the superior what it is. However, the interviewer should not give up. He can rephrase his question, ask a similiar question, or try to probe deeper. Examples are: "Can you suggest any improvements we might try?" "What things have not been changed by the new system that might be causing some difficulty?" "Are any of our people having problems?" "How do you feel about our packaging methods?"

Inadequate responses closely parallel irrelevant ones. There are several reasons why the respondent would give inadequate responses. He may not be sure how much information you want; he may not understand the question; or he may not know the answer. It is important that the interviewer recognize inadequate answers so that additional questions can be posed. Examples of inadequate answers are:

Interviewer: How do you feel about our new project?
Interviewee: Sometimes I really find it challenging.
Interviewer: How did you like your last job?
Interviewee: I was really excited about it at first.

Frequently the inexperienced interviewer unknowingly asks leading or loaded questions. These questions make it easy, if not necessary, for the respondent to answer in a particular way. Examples are: "You like your work, don't you?" "Most workers are not in favor of unionism, and you're probably not either, are you?" "Don't you feel you owe your loyalty to a company like this which has so many benefits for its employees?" "Do you consider yourself hard working or lazy?" These questions will not get the respondent's true feelings and thus are of no value whatsoever.

Using questions in an interview is a very complex process. It requires the interviewer to listen carefully so that he gets the kind of information he can use. Some respondents try to "read" the interviewer and feed him the answer that he might want to hear. This can be done by analyzing the direction of the questions and checking closely for nonverbal indications. A neutral question can become biased if the interviewer emphasizes a particular word or phrase. The respondent who is trying to please the interviewer can use this as an indication of the kind of response desired. The good interviewer knows the types of questions to ask and how to ask them.

The Phases of an Interview

There are five phases into which the interview process may be divided. By understanding these continuous phases, the interviewer can develop effective strategies.

1. Preliminary Planning. Although planning is not a part of the actual interview, the lack of adequate planning is found in many studies to be the greatest single fault of an interview. Included in this phase is identifying the objective to be achieved. The individual to be interviewed should be notified of the objective and points to be covered. Preliminary information should be obtained and the time and place of the interview scheduled. A brief written outline of strategic questions and points can be used to guide the interview and to help the interviewer decide on the amount of structure necessary to accomplish his objective.

2. Opening. How quickly an individual actively participates in an interview may be determined by the initial face-to-face contact. An interview which begins on a tone of friendliness and helpfulness is off to a good start. Privacy is essential, and the interviewer who indicates that there are to be no interruptions has gone a long way toward establishing rapport with the interviewee.

Rapport is essential to a good interview. Since every courtesy is greatly magnified in the eyes of the interviewee, any attempt to put him at ease is noticed. Methods of establishing rapport generally include smiling, small talk, offering cigarettes or coffee, and explaining the need for items such as pens and notepads to be used in the interview.

Another characteristic of the opening phase is to state the purpose of the interview. Charles Stewart and William Cash have identified a number of "attention getting" or "orientation" statements they call starters. They are: (1) summarizing the problem; (2) explaining how the problem was discovered; (3) mentioning an incentive or reward for taking part in an interview; (4) requesting advice or assistance; (5) referring, if known, to the interviewee's position on an issue; (6) referring to the person who suggested the interviewee; (7) referring to the organization one represents; and (8) requesting a specified period of time.

The opening of an interview is usually short but it establishes rapport and provides an understanding of purpose. This phase is important as it may determine how productive the remainder of the interview is.

3. Body. This, of course, is the bulk of the interview. In a thirty-minute interview, twenty-five minutes may be allotted to this phase. The skills of the interviewer for guiding the conversation, developing information, and analyzing the data are used to accomplish his purpose.

Guiding the conversation should be easy for the interviewer. Small inflections of the voice can be used to give encouragement. Phases can be repeated to get the respondent to give additional details. Restating the reply allows time for reflection and clarification of a point. Nodding can be used to encourage the interviewee when he is giving useful information. Semivocal expressions such as "Umm . . . ," which have no direct interpretation, can be received as the interviewee wants to receive them. A brief summarizing statement from time to time provides clarity and serves to keep both the interviewer and interviewee aware of the direction of the interview.

Too often the inexperienced interviewer puts forth another question while the respondent is still struggling to find adequate words to use in responding to a previous question. People get a distorted sense of time during an interview and this heightens their fear of silence. To measure this sense of distorted time, a study was conducted in which a conversation was stopped for a short period. Interviewers' estimates of the period of silence magnified it by a factor of from 10 to 100. Conversely, there are some indications that interviewees tend to underestimate the time elapsed. Thus, the interviewer should be aware of this distortion and not push forward too rapidly.

The format of an interview, involving as it usually does a conversation between two people, is demanding of both participants. Not only must the interviewer guide, direct, probe, but he must also listen carefully and attentively to the responses, both verbal and nonverbal. He must constantly be alert to hearing only what he wants to hear. Each of us filters out certain information and ranks the value of other information. As a result of this process, the interviewer needs to be certain that his impression is an accurate impression. This can be achieved by building in feedback questions: "It is my understanding that . . ." or "What I hear you saying is . . . ."

In most interviews questions are asked by the interviewee as the conversation progresses. Especially in the employment interview, for example, the applicant should be given opportunity and encouragement to ask questions about the company, the position for which he is applying, and other issues. The interviewer should respond to these questions in a clear, specific manner. If the question is about what hours the interviewee would work, the answer is easy, but if the question is what has the company done to protect the environment, the answer may be quite involved. Nevertheless, it is one's responsibility to answer any question as completely and thoroughly as possible.

4. Closing. This phase of the interview is perhaps the most important in that the relevant points or decisions reached during the interview are recited. Where subsequent activities were agreed to, these are reviewed. Studies indicate that vital information which was not revealed in the body of the interview may be mentioned in closing. Essentially both people leave the interview with a clear understanding of what was agreed to and what action is to be taken.

5. Follow-up. Depending on the type of interview undertaken, one needs some kind of follow-up. In those where decisions were made, the follow-up would be a memorandum or letter. Where a number of decisions were reached, the follow-up would be a list of actions to be taken. The follow-up insures maximum benefits from the interview.

These phases of the interview show that it has a definite structure regardless of the content or purpose of the discussion. In business organizations the interview is a popular technique, used for many different purposes, which determine its type.

THE INFORMATION-SEEKING INTERVIEW

Whatever the setting, executive suite or construction site, the purpose of the information-seeking interview is the same: to get information as accurately and completely as possible in the shortest amount of time. Too often we assume that this is a simple process and too often we fail.

In order to obtain the relevant and valid data that are necessary, the interviewer should identify the general purpose of the interview and then outline what information is necessary for him to obtain in order to achieve his purpose. By proceeding step-by-step he will be able to conduct a successful interview.

Stewart and Cash suggest that the first step in preparing the informational interview is to delimit the purpose or purposes of the interview. First, why do we want to conduct the interview(s)? The second step—determining specific objectives—is a further delimiting process. Both short and long range goals of the interview and what the interview will require of the respondents should be considered. An appropriate structure for the interview should be selected. How much should the interviewer control the discussion? How much time should be allotted to the interview? What types of questions will elicit the most meaningful information?

Information-seeking interviews can be used to discover attitudes, aspirations, fears, values, beliefs as well as opinions, knowledge, and skill. Many conversations between superior-subordinate could be more productive if both parties realized they were engaged in an information-seeking interview.

Persuasive Interview

Perhaps the most difficult of all interviews, the persuasive interview has as its purpose the changing of a person's behavior. Every day we encounter numerous persuasive interviews although we might not recognize them as such. Any exchange with a salesman is conducted in the context of a persuasive interview. In much the same way we go through our routine in the organization trying to convince others of the significance and desirability of our ideas, concepts, plans, and suggestions.

Persuasion is difficult because it demands change. Studies indicate that a key to effective persuasive interviewing is the appeal to the interests of the interviewee. The interviewer must show how the person being interviewed will benefit from making the desired decision or change. Since most of us tend to hang tenaciously to our beliefs and behavior, persuading another person to change is not easy.

The interviewer can enhance his possibilities of success if he appeals to a need, illustrates that his proposal is feasibile, and emphasizes the benefits of the proposal. One's success is enhanced if he knows who the interviewee is and how to appeal to him. It may be necessary to gather all relevant information about the person to be persuaded. The values of the person and his relevance to the proposal are of particular interest to the interviewer. The persuader should determine which values might be of use to him in his persuasion strategy and to determine when and how to use them.

Additionally the interviewer should be aware of the other person's viewpoint. Are the changes under consideration threatening to him? In what ways? Does he perceive you as someone who is shaking up the establishment? Would he prefer another course of action? What effect will the change under consideration have on his day-to-day routine? Does he trust your leadership? Will he lose power if the change is implemented? Has he been misinformed? All of these aspects need to be considered for the interviewer to understand his opposition and to plan how to persuade him to change.

Attention should be paid to the setting in which the persuasive interview takes place. For example, are you to sit behind your desk, in front of someone else's desk, or face to face in chairs? Is the room private? Is the setting formal or informal? Will there be interruptions? Timing and setting are important considerations in the persuasive interview. The best time to ask for a raise is obviously after one has earned distinction and the best setting may be on neutral ground, such as the golf course or a restaurant.

The best way to argue a persuasive case is to be prepared with reasons, evidence, and data. There are several types of information that can be used: specific examples, factual illustration, hypothetical illustration, comparisons, statistics, and testimony by experts.

The strategy used to convince the interviewee depends on the person, setting, and topic. Most often used are strategies which employ a common belief approach. This appeals to common interests or beliefs shared by the interviewer and interviewee. Frequently this is expanded to the "however stage" where the interviewer outlines the differences and proceeds to reciting his arguments. It is generally agreed that the strongest point can be used at the beginning or end with effectiveness but should never be given in the middle. The climax order, or main point last, seems to have a slight edge in terms of persuasive effectiveness.

The good persuasive interview takes into account the objective, person, setting, strategy, and situation. All communication skills, listening as well as talking, are used in the effective persuasive interview.

EMPLOYMENT INTERVIEW

The employment interview, probably more than any other type of interview, reflects the complexities of the communication process. Studies have shown that the answers depend on the questions; that what the interviewer hears depends on what his attitude is; that one interviewer hears one thing while another hears something else although they are both given the same information; that bad information is remembered longer than good; that the earlier the bad information the more importance it is given; and that interviewers make up their mind very early in the interview, usually based on stereotypes of "good candidates."

Why then, with all of these difficulties, is the employment interview still used by organizations? Because it best fills a number of purposes.

In addition to the screening process, the interviewer must

convey information about the job and the organization. Also, the interviewer should promote good will for the organization. Since not all applicants are hired, it may be particularly important that the interviewer create a favorable impression of the organization.

It is important that the interviewer be prepared for the interview by setting aside a sufficient amount of time for the process, studying the written application, and noting the questions he will ask. The interviewee is always distressed by being asked questions which can be answered by the interviewer's glancing at his application. It communicates that he is not being considered seriously or is not worthy of a few minutes of your time. The closing of the interview should always include a description of the next procedure so the interviewee will have a clear understanding of what to expect.

While it has been estimated that as many as 150 million employment interviews occur in the United States every year, it is not a procedure without problems. Too often the interviewer makes up his mind prematurely on "facts" that are likely to sound totally different to another interviewer. Thus, many organizations are using more than one interviewer to help offset these communication difficulties. By being aware of basic communication principles, the employment interviewer can do a better job of selecting the right person for the position.

APPRAISAL INTERVIEW

A new manager began face-to-face meetings with each of his staff members. Word quickly spread that he was conducting performance or appraisal interviews and every employee was to be called in for evaluation. Of the three people interviewed the first morning, every one left with the understanding that he was to soon be promoted! Weeks later when one of these employees asked the supervisor when the promotion would be announced, the new manager indicated that had not been his understanding of their conversation and a promotion was not under consideration. The result was a hostile, confused staff.

What went wrong? Probably the performance or appraisal interview contributes to more misunderstandings than any other. The manager's goal was to reassure his staff that he had no intention of firing anyone and was prepared to reward those whom he felt were making the largest contributions to the goals of the organization. The staff, with little previous experience at communicating with the new boss, had completely misinterpreted his remarks. The result was a massive communication breakdown.

While the appraisal interview is usually associated with letting the employee know what management thinks of his performance, it is not limited to that single purpose. N. R. F. Maler lists eight goals of appraisal, each of which may be appropriate depending on circumstances:

1. To let the subordinate know where he stands.
2. To recognize good work by the subordinate.
3. To point out how the subordinate can improve.
4. To develop the subordinate in his present job.
5. To develop or train the subordinate for a higher level job.
6. To let the subordinate know how to progress in the organization.
7. To serve as a record, showing how the subordinate fits into the organization.
8. To issue a formal warning to the subordinate that he must improve.

Since the appraisal interview is often conducted in a highly emotional climate, the interviewer can begin the session by indicating which of these various goals will be covered in the interview. The superior must adapt his style to the subordinates being interviewed. Obviously rapport will be more easily established with one than another and some are going to be more anxious than others. Since the impression an interview makes is often determined more by how the interview is handled than by what is said, the successful interviewer modifies his style according to the person.

The focus of the interview should always be on why things are as they are and how they can be improved in the future. Research indicates that employees perform best when asked to set their own goals. The more the subordinate is involved in the appraisal process the greater the improvement in the superior-subordinate relationship.

CORRECTION INTERVIEW

One of the most amusing stories of a man who was called in for a correction interview involves the quality supervisor of a company that makes rum cakes. As the Christmas season was approaching the man was assigned to calculate the amount of rum to be included in each cake. New on the job and inexperienced at making such determinations, the man worked diligently on his calculations until he felt confident they were accurate. Approval was given to make the line changes necessary to produce the rum cakes ordered for the Christmas season. In a fifteen-minute period the line produced several hundred rum cakes when the discovery was made that each cake had fifteen times the amount of rum necessary!

The correction interview that followed had a definite threat of dismissal coupled with an intense curiosity as to how anyone could miscalculate that amount of rum. This, of course, was not a typical correction interview.

Generally the purpose of the correction interview is the identification of undesirable behavior and the correction of that difficulty. A correction interview should always be scheduled as soon as possible following the violation. It is necessary for the interviewer to be prepared with facts and proposals for corrective action. Of course, it is helpful to involve the employee in determining appropriate action, but this may not always be possible.

The interviewer who uses a moderately nondirective style often obtains the best results. The general structure is an outline of the alleged violation, a request that the subordinate explain his version of the incident and a proposal of corrective action. At the end of the interview a summary of the decisions should be given and a description of what follow-up action will be taken.

GRIEVANCE INTERVIEW

One method of improving communication in the organization is the provision of a grievance interview aimed at resolving employee complaints. Through this interview the employee's frustrations can be explained and acted upon. Often these interviews are highly emotional since the employee may not have registered his complaint immediately but may have brooded about the alleged injustice for some time. Thus, the interviewer should be prepared to hear an emotional outburst.

The interviewer should open the discussion by outlining the purpose of the interview and stating his intention to listen carefully and provide as satisfactory a solution as is possible. Following the discussion of the grievance, the interviewer should close by reviewing any decisions made, and how they are to be achieved.

EXIT INTERVIEW

Whenever employees voluntarily leave the organization, an exit interview may be conducted. The purpose of this interview is to determine why the employee decided to leave, to promote good will, and to demonstrate appreciation for the work done by the employee.

Recent studies have revealed that the exit interview is usually not successful in accomplishing these objectives. Too often the departing employee is not frank and open about why he is leaving. Fear of receiving a poor recommendation is probably the main reason the exiting employee is less than truthful.

Some organizations have modified their procedures to allow for this occurrence. By sending questionnaires to the employee's home and guaranteeing his anonymity, information can be obtained that the exit interview did not elicit. By waiting until the employee is working at another job, the interviewer is able to gather valuable information about why the employee was unhappy or discontent.

CAUSES OF INEFFECTIVE INTERVIEWS

There is considerable agreement on the two most common causes of information being distorted in an interview. These are interviewer bias and lack of empathy by the interviewer.

Interviewer bias has been defined as unwanted or unplanned interviewer influence in the interview process. Too often the interviewer's background clearly influences the way he perceives people and situations. That is, we hear what we want to hear. Particularly interviews which lack structure permit considerable influence by the interviewer's personal characteristics.

In order to allow for this interviewer bias, care should be taken in the wording of questions, and the interviewer should plan the direction that the interview is to take. By being aware of interviewer bias, the individual may be able to recognize bias and take corrective action.

Another cause of ineffective interviews is a lack of empathy by the interviewer. Empathy simply refers to one's ability to put himself in the other person's shoes. It means that the interviewer must not be content to just listen to the words and meaning but must try to identify with the interviewee's emotions, values, and attitudes. When the interviewee believes that he is being understood, the interview is highly productive. However, if he believes that the interviewer is not understanding what he is saying and why, the interview accomplishes little. Lack of empathy often causes ineffective interviews because empathy is an important ingredient in any exchange.

CHECK LIST FOR CONDUCTING A GOOD INTERVIEW

The following check list is offered for helping the interviewer plan and conduct an effective interview.

Preliminary Planning:
Has the objective been identified?
Has the interviewee been notified of the objective and points to be covered?
Has all preliminary information been obtained and read?
Have the time and place of the interview been scheduled?
What strategic questions should be asked?
How much structure is necessary?

Opening:
How is rapport to be established?
How can I appear to be at ease?
Has a statement of purpose been adequately prepared?

Body:
How can the interviewee be encouraged to participate to the fullest extent possible?
What logical procedure is to be used?

What methods of guiding the conversation can be used?
How can summarizing statements best be utilized?
Will probing questions be necessary?
How can feedback be used to increase effectiveness?
Am I prepared to answer questions that the interviewee might have?

Closing:
What subsequent activities may be agreed to?
How can the relevant points of decisions be summarized?
What friendly, constructive note can the interview end on?

Follow-Up:
Will a written follow-up be necessary or helpful?
What follow-up action would maximize the benefits obtained by the
interview?
What can be learned from this interview that will help one conduct
better interviews in the future?

Today's administrator needs effective interviewing skills in order to accomplish his goals. Fortunately interviewing skills need not be difficult to obtain. By being aware of the *parts of an interview*, types of interviews, interviewer bias and need for empathy, the manager or administrator can increase his effectiveness.

7

A COMMUNICATION FORMULA FOR GOOD LEADERSHIP

There is nothing more difficult to take in hand, more perilous to conduct, or more uncertain in its success, than to take the lead in the introduction of a new order of things.

Machiavelli

Leadership, that often used but little understood term, is a form of power. It is the art of influencing, directing, and motivating people through persuasion to follow you. It is persuasive power and not coercion.

A number of myths surround the concept of leadership. Probably the greatest of these is that some people are born leaders. The truth is leadership is learned and earned and is not a birthright. Actually leadership is a function of personality traits, the situation at hand, and the resulting interaction or the style an individual adopts when attempting to lead. These three elements of leadership are of course all fused together through communication.

Too many people, if placed in a position to lead, assume that they show leadership by barking out orders and making lonely decisions. The error here is that such a person equates coercive power with the behaviors of a leader. A person may give orders and make decisions due to the position he holds in the organization, but he is not leading.

As noted earlier, true leadership stems from persuasive power. This does not mean the form of persuasion of laughing and slapping people on the back—that's salesmanship. Persuasive power as

99

a communication concept refers to the potential of an individual's influence on other people whether they are subordinates, co-workers, superiors, or a peer group in the organization.

Leaders do many things. They do make decisions, offer suggestions, plan, solve problems, enforce policies and rules, and influence others with their ideas. But primarily what they do is motivate.

As you take on more responsibility in your job, you will have to do a better job of selecting and motivating others to accomplish your objectives. Through persuasion you will have to motivate them to follow your direction and adopt your ideas, and often this involves changing attitudes. To do this will require leadership on your part—a trade that has to be learned. The learning takes place when you realize that leadership doesn't go with the title. It is earned. And while you may be well-liked by those around you, if you can't improve the performance of your group, you are not an effective leader.

To be a good leader you have to be more than efficient, you have to be *effective*. A person's leadership is measured by what he achieves, not necessarily by what he does. The bottom line is *output*, not input. This means that many people are efficient but not effective and hence do not reveal true leadership. It is the leader's job to be effective—to accomplish the organization's objectives.

I once worked with a man who thought he had great leadership ability. He was always at his desk, worked on weekends, followed orders, kept elaborate files, and was friendly. In short, he was concerned with doing things right, but he never considered if he was doing the right things. Year after year younger men were promoted over him because what he was doing was irrelevant to effectiveness and hence leadership. Neither he nor his followers ever accomplished much because they confused results with behavior or effectiveness with efficiency.

Consequently, whatever style leadership assumes, it is a means for meeting objectives, which requires skills. An effective leader realizes that in different circumstances different leadership styles are called for. The trick is to identify which style would be the most effective under the particular circumstances. There is no single best way to lead effectively in all situations. The conclusion is that since situations vary so much, so must leadership style. Research by social scientists and business scholars as well as common sense support this conclusion.

However, if you are in a leadership position you still have to adopt some type of style and lead. How do you know if it is appropriate?

The answer, although not easy, is found in the earlier formula:

Leadership = f(traits, situation, interaction).

That is, leadership is a function of personality traits, the situation at hand, and the resulting interaction or the style an individual adopts when attempting to lead. Each of these leadership elements will be discussed individually.

TRAIT RESEARCH

Early studies of leadership argued that what makes a leader effective is some set of built-in personality traits. The trait theory school searched for common traits such as "independence," "friendliness," "aggressiveness," or "optimism," that all leaders possessed.

After years of research the evidence is clear: leadership is far too complex to be reduced to a set of traits. Such an attempt to build a model of leadership based on traits failed because most of the research was done in the artificial environment of the laboratory rather than in the rough and tumble world of the organization; followers often had the same traits as leaders; no common traits could be found for all leaders; and finally the particular situation has a major impact upon leadership.

Despite the failure of this trait theory research, it is clear that the work uncovered a valuable lesson: a person's personality is a major factor in determining leadership. One's personality, which may be viewed generally as a set of traits, does influence one's behavior and this behavior affects those around you in terms of whether they will follow or resist you.

While any statement that says, "leaders must always have the following traits . . . ," is false, it is true that certain traits are more likely to be found in leaders than others. Decades of research add up to these final traits of the leader's personality:

A strong desire—almost an obsession—to be a winner. This means that while the price of winning may be extremely high the leader will pay it—usually in the form of hard work. When reviewing the resumés of leaders who have won it is obvious that they have made winning a habit. They avoid losing like it was a contagious disease. Apparently they would agree with the former baseball great, Leo Durocher, who said, "You show me a good loser and I'll show you a loser."

Conviction. Leaders have the strength to see a difficult task through. This does not mean charging blindly into the cannon fire, but it does mean being forceful, providing an example and setting the pace. Leaders display their convictions through intelligent positive action rather than through negative defeating attitudes.

Responsibility. For a group to be loyal and supportive their leader must accept his share of the blame when things go wrong rather than trying to say the goof was their fault. Leaders are not afraid of responsibility, in fact, they welcome it because they realize it gives them an opportunity for accomplishing their goals. I once knew the head of an organization who began all of his departmental meetings with the question, "What's the bad news?" He explained that he did this "because I need the bad news the worst," meaning he wanted as much time as possible to deal with the problem. His departmental heads were always open and candid with him because they knew he would not yell and scream at them, but would accept his share of the responsibility for solving the difficulty.

Knowledgeable. To lead, an individual must have the technical skills required for the job and current information so as to remain relevant. Information and understanding are power and every leader understands this. It is reported that Paul Lyet, chief executive of Sperry Rand, in his climb to the top would visit headquarters once a month to report on his division's progress with his briefcase bulging with reports and ledgers. Others at the meeting found his appearance comical, but the snickering soon stopped as Lyet sat down to deliver his report. Fact after fact rolled out and through this preparation he gained the respect of those at the meeting and ultimately those in top management at Sperry. In short, Lyet got to the top by doing his homework better than anyone else.

Foresight. Leaders develop an ability for predicting future events and reacting accordingly. Planning is essential if one is going to lead because the future can be invented. That is, decisions made today determine what decisions have to be made later. Leaders do not enjoy dealing with a crisis—they much prefer to deal with planned events because the outcome can be controlled. While leaders may be good at solving crises because of their other skills, they do not want to play the role of a fireman. They realize that through planning most of these fires could have been prevented.

On the negative side, trait theory research has identified several characteristics that prevent one from being a leader.

Probably the most damaging trait is fear. This fear may reveal itself in many forms. Fear of superiors, subordinates, coworkers, government, lawsuits, the press, and so forth, whether real or imagined, keeps the individual from acting assertively and leading. This trait is so fatal to a potential leader because so much energy, practically all of it, is used up worrying, fighting ghosts, marshalling forces for an attack that never comes, and seeing some sinister motive in the behavior of others. As a result the individual has no chance to lead because there is no time for positive planning and goal setting with all of his resources used to defend against these fears. Certainly this is not to say there is nothing to fear in organizational life, but the leader knows the difference between the real and the imagined and acts accordingly.

Coupled with the damaging trait of neurotic fear is indecisiveness in decision making. A person with this trait of indecisiveness can't lead because all of his time is spent trying to decide what to do. With the pressure on and time running out he usually grabs in desperation some solution and usually it is the wrong one. Or he waits until events overtake him so that in reality, with his options gone, the decision is made for him. Nowhere is the lack of leadership more evident than when the boss won't decide on a crucial matter. Ultimately if he won't decide on a course of action, he has in fact decided because life won't stop. Others will begin to behave based on his lack of behavior, and decisions will be made up and down the line.

I once knew a departmental head who could never decide on which secretary to hire. As the weeks passed without a replacement, life in the department went on with negative results as the other secretaries had to take up the slack, appointments were missed, phone calls were not returned, and morale dropped. With his inability to decide between person A and B he had in fact made a second decision—not to hire anyone—with negative effects upon the whole department. This also underscores the point that indecisiveness may occur at any level of decision making and is not confined to major decisions.

This does not mean that leaders always make quick decisions. On the contrary, they may spend considerable time before deciding, but the point is that they do decide. By being decisive, leaders are able to be reflective rather than reflexive in their decision making.

The Situational Context

As was noted earlier fifty years of research has not produced a single set of traits that, if possessed by a person, will guarantee him to be a leader. This is true because traits are usually viewed in isolation while a leader must interact with those being led in a particular *situation*. Now we are ready to discuss the second factor in our leadership formula, the situational context.

In considering the situation as having an effect upon someone emerging as a leader one realizes that many things are part of the situation. For example, such factors as size of the organization or department, the particular problem to be dealt with, social climate, time, norms and roles, and power are all important in determining whether leadership will develop and from whom. Because all of them influence anyone attempting to lead in a particular situation the conclusion is reached, after years of research, that leadership is relative to the situational context.

The sheer size of the organization or department affects one's ability to lead. It is much easier to cause change with a few people than many. Lyndon Johnson was very effective in persuading people when face to face with them, but ineffective when talking to the people via national television.

The problem at hand can vary from leading an evacuation crew at a mine disaster to heading a team of research scientists at an R&D firm on a project with each problem calling for a different form of leadership.

Certainly if you were asked to head a group of employees it would affect your leadership ability if they were friendly or hostile toward you.

Time is a crucial situational factor because you may have to take immediate action if disaster is imminent or if you have months to get a feel for the job.

It pays the person attempting to exert leadership to remember that one is not free to do anything, but is limited to a great extent by the role he is in and the norms of the group. If a person violates these it is doubtful that he will ever be an effective leader.

Finally, there is the important factor of power in the situation. If you are attempting to lead but have little power, your chances of succeeding are lessened because those around you realize you can't deliver rewards or punishment. Those being led have to believe that you have a carrot or a stick.

In summary, leadership depends as much upon the situation as it does upon the leader's own personality traits. Because of the situational context it doesn't make much sense to speak of someone as a "born leader."

The Third Element: Interaction

Remember in our formula for leadership a third factor, interaction, was listed. This third element is most important when you consider the leader as a communicator. In the give and take of the organization, leadership is a kind of interaction between people. This interaction is in the form of communication—both verbal and nonverbal—and we may refer to it as the style of leadership. Here the focus will be on what leaders do rather than on their personal traits.

Over the years much research has been conducted on various leadership styles and how they influence different kinds of interaction between leaders and followers. Basically the research has generated three common leadership styles. They are:

1.   autocratic, authoritarian, or supervisory
2.   democratic, consultive, or participatory
3.   laissez-faire or free reign.

The *autocratic leader* gets obedience from his followers by the use of formal authority, rewards, and punishment. He runs a tight ship by setting all policy and making all the decisions. It is clear to him what he wants done, and he makes it quite clear to his followers what their work assignments are.

The advantages of the autocratic style when leading are that it can be an efficient way of getting things done, it saves time and is often effective in a crisis situation when quick decisions and a clear chain of command are needed. It also has the advantage of appealing to employees who aren't used to making decisions and fear uncertainty in work roles, and who feel most secure when given direct work orders to follow.

However, there are disadvantages to the autocratic style. The chief weakness is that it is based on a one-way communication channel—from boss to subordinates. Without a feedback loop from the followers, errors and misunderstanding often result. Linked to this lack of feedback is a second weakness, singular decision making by the autocrat. In today's complex organization such decision making by one person is risky. A third disadvantage is that satisfaction from the work group is usually the lowest under an autocrat because people like to feel involved and have some say as to what happens in the work environment.

The *democratic leader* asks for ideas and suggestions from his followers. He encourages and invites them to participate to some degree. In some instances, he may let the group decide policy and he will abide by it. In others he asks for their advice but makes it clear he will make the final decision. In either case the followers are given more freedom and participation than under the autocratic style.

The advantages to the democratic style are increased worker satisfaction, group cohesiveness, and better communication between boss and subordinates. In addition efficiency often improves because when people help make a decision or understand why something is being done they often work harder to see that it is done correctly. Also because of the increased communications the leader has the benefit of more information, ideas, talent, and experience from his people. Also it gives the leader on the rise in the organization a chance to view his subordinates as a possible replacement for him because he has observed them under fire due to their increased freedom to act.

As with any style there are disadvantages. It can be inefficient and time consuming as followers thrash out ideas on a problem. As with any style that delegates authority to followers, it can result in the loss of managerial control by the leader. Also the leader that uses this style must be sure that he wants and will use the ideas of his followers (if practical) otherwise they will turn resentful if their suggestions are constantly ignored.

The *laissez-faire or free-reign leader* plays down his role and generally serves to provide information, materials, and goals for his subordinates. This does not mean that he turns all control over to his followers, but that he does exercise a minimum of control over them. Often he sets the goals for the group along with deadlines and budget, but he leaves it up to them to develop the "how" to get the job done. Thus the subordinates are free to operate without much direction from the leader unless they ask for it.

The largest advantage of this leadership style is that it does give followers complete freedom to act. Many highly trained employees produce only at top efficiency when given this level of motivation from management to act. For such a work force this type of style results in high work satisfaction.

The free-reign style does have its disadvantages. It allows the leader little control over his followers. This lack of control carries a high degree of risk if goals and objectives can't be met. To use this style, a leader must know his people well, their abilities and honesty.

The conclusion to be drawn from research and working managers is that there is no single best leadership style for all situations. Experienced leaders know they have a choice of leadership styles and the real art of leadership is being able to identify which style is most appropriate under particular circumstances.

To the question "Is the autocratic style better than the democratic?" the best answer is "Not necessarily." Any "best" style for exerting leadership will depend on the individual's personality. Usually a leader assumes a style unconsciously which is reflective of his personality.

Also the particular employees and their attitudes play a significant role in determining which style is best. As a general rule subordinates who don't know a great deal about the overall task at hand need a leadership style that is work-oriented or autocratic. On the other hand, subordinates who have a good understanding of the task need a leadership style that is employee-oriented or democratic or perhaps even laissez-faire. The bottom line is that leadership style is too complex to be reduced to a single "best" style. In fact, research findings as well as work experiences indicate that an effective leader probably assumes all three styles depending on the circumstances. Sometimes this runs contrary to his personality, but he realizes job effectiveness depends on flexibility when leading. There are times such as meeting a critical deadline that he has to assume the autocratic style, and other times, particularly when planning strategy, that a style such as the democratic is most appropriate.

Thus social science research and on-the-job practices offer views on leadership style, but there is a third perspective for discussing this complicated subject—the viewpoint of those being led. What style do they prefer to follow?

Style Preferences of Subordinates

Interviews with subordinates tend to show that they prefer a leader who leans toward the democratic or participative style. Subordinates tend to think that the democratic leader is more effective than the autocratic because of particular behaviors he exhibits. Some of these are:

1. The democratic leader shares information with his subordinates thereby keeping them more informed and making them feel more secure. They feel they know what is going on and can have some say about their work environment.
2. He communicates with them more freely creating an atmosphere of understanding.
3. He listens to their problems and helps when he can.
4. He provides support for his subordinates. Some of this takes the form of personal help, but also includes getting things for them in the organization such as better working conditions, office space, travel money, and clerical help.
5. He shows confidence in his subordinates by asking them for advice on a sticky problem and using their suggestions. However, he tends to retain the final decision for himself.
6. He concentrates on rewarding rather than punishing subordinates. Rewards, economic or social, are used to motivate followers and punishment is rarely used because people tend to repeat behaviors that are rewarded and discontinue behaviors that fail to get rewarded. The practical lesson here is that subordinates are more likely to be motivated by rewards than punishment. Mistakes, rather than resulting in punishment, are used by the leader as a learning experience to train the employee. Poor performance is not used as a basis for punishment.

In addition, there is more information from subordinates that most prefer to work under a leader who is more democratic than autocratic. Some of their reasons follow.

The democratic leader encourages cooperation. The effective democratic leader being pragmatic knows that he can get his subordinates to work by using his authority, or he can motivate them to be self-starters. Realistically he sometimes has to use his authority, but most of the time he relies on motivation through rewards rather than punishment.

A truly effective leader has the power to reward his followers.

Often the reward can be a pay increase, but this may not be the most important. In many instances noneconomic rewards are most effective in motivating subordinates to excel. One that many effective leaders use is recognition for a job well done. This can be a simple "thank you" or a memo to go in the employee's file or an invitation to discuss some ideas with the leader.

The democratic leader is consistent. The effective leader maintains consistent behavior while on the job and shows patience and understanding toward his subordinates. If subordinates feel they can predict how the boss will react to problems they will feel more secure and can act more freely, but if they have a boss who is unpredictable and may suddenly lash out at them then they will be overly cautious, offer few suggestions, and tend to hide when problems arise rather than helping to solve them.

On the negative side subordinates reflect some very definite ideas or complaints about their leader. Here are some of the most common.

1. He never plans and is always disorganized. This is usually seen as, or takes the form of, crisis management due to the lack of planning. For example, everything is slow Monday through Thursday and then on Friday it's rush, rush, rush in order to meet a Monday deadline.
2. He fails to reward. A common complaint is, "I've worked for him for sixteen years, and I've had to beg for every raise I ever got and never once have I received a thank you." This typical complaint offers plenty of advice for someone wanting to be an effective leader; reward your subordinates when they do a good job so they will know you saw and appreciated it. This reward may be financial or social and quite often subordinates will eventually expect both.
3. He never gives credit to employees. This complaint is usually found when the boss won't recognize that a subordinate had a good idea, or that the boss made a mistake, or tells subordinates how to perform a task they have been doing well for five years. Subordinates resent any boss who acts as though they don't have a brain. Often they complain that the insensitive leader treats his followers as though they were objects like typewriters or desk calculators. This is an excellent way to humiliate subordinates and foster antiboss hostility.

An effective leader avoids these common complaints because he realizes whether real or imaginary a serious complaint has to be dealt with. If a subordinate thinks a problem exists then he will behave accordingly, and in reality a problem does then exist that has to be solved.

In conclusion the complexity of leadership styles does not point to a single answer. However, a general pattern does emerge for the person trying to exert leadership in the organization of today. An important difference between the authoritarian, autocratic style and the more participative, democratic is in the number of different roles or behaviors each allows when interacting with subordinates. The leader following the autocratic style has fewer ways of dealing with subordinates. Basically he has to rely on his role as an authority due to the position he holds. It is difficult for him to shift from this role. He is much like the lion tamer who must rely on the whip and chair for getting the job done. But the democratic (more participative) leader is able to adopt many different roles as the need arises and can slide up and down the scale from boss to one of the guys. His strength as leader lies in his flexibility when dealing with workers. In light of the complex differences among employees in a large organization today, the more flexible posture a leader can assume without giving up his authority the more likely he will be able to lead effectively.

Only after examining the formula given earlier for effective leadership can a person decide what is the best leadership style for him to adopt given the time and the situation.

One of the most deadly things a leader can do in an organizational setting is to become isolated. The disease is known as executive isolation. It is most commonly found among executives using the autocratic leadership style. In essence executive isolation occurs when a leader loses contact with his subordinates so that he really doesn't know what's happening in his department or organization. For someone charged with leading this disease can be fatal. Another reason it is dangerous to a leader is that he usually doesn't know he has it until it's too late. Here are some typical examples of a leader becoming isolated.

A department manager has a turnover rate of 50 percent yearly among employees but doesn't know why.

A director of employee relations learns of a pending strike at the plant from his morning newspaper.

A store manager is surprised to learn of a steady decrease in sales for the past year.

A president of a large corporation keeps losing young articulate middle managers to smaller firms although he has no idea why they keep leaving.

A president keeps getting glowing fiscal reports from his departmental heads only to find the books in the red at the end of the fiscal year.

The major cause of this trouble is due to a leader being a poor communicator. Peter Drucker, the top management consultant in the nation, says that a leader is going to become isolated if he views communication as flowing from the top down in an organization from the supervisor to the subordinates. A leader with this viewpoint of organizational communication is not really listening so that information never rises from the bottom to the top. By not staying in touch with the rank and file, a leader can't take the pulse of his people. One executive says, "Nine out of ten complaints boil down to poor communications—management's inability to get to the roots of what motivates and demotivates people."

Many leaders announce an "open-door" policy for dealing with subordinates, yet few people stop by to talk. This open-door policy may actually be a closed one. If your people are afraid to talk to you about problems or bring bad news because you snap at them, then in effect you have slammed the door in their face. The closed-door boss may also achieve this unpopular image by having his office guarded by a secretary. This type often remarks that he can't get his paper work done because people keep interrupting him. Through his isolation he is headed for trouble and he doesn't even know it.

J. Paul Lyet, chief executive of Sperry Rand Corporation, works hard to create a spirit of openness at Sperry now that he has the top. To achieve this he makes his office a place where division presidents can talk about their mistakes and problems without being upbraided. He says, "I like to feel there's an ease of communication. I like to feel that the division presidents can come in here, and their mouths aren't dry. You don't dress people down in front of other people, you don't treat executives like your children—you don't even treat your children like that."

Fortunately the disease of executive isolation can be cured if caught in time. Usually a leader has a chance when he takes over his new role to set up channels of communication to his subordinates thereby preventing or curing the disease. He can take certain steps to let everyone know that he will not be cut off from them. Here are some ways to keep from being isolated.

1. Assume you may have lost contact with your subordinates. This gives you the proper attitude for seeing the communications problem for what it is. Kay C. Lambeth, president, Erwin-Lambeth, Inc., a Southern custom furniture maker, says, a leader must understand that the reading of the pulse of one's people is a number one priority. Also remember as you get more people under you the natural tendency is to lose close contact with them.
2. Get out of the office and talk with your subordinates in their work areas. This sounds easy but most leaders forget to do it, so schedule this activity on your calendar for once a week—even if it is only a thirty-minute meeting. This is what Edward E. Carlson did when he took over United Airlines to solve a tremendous morale problem among employees.
3. Schedule informal meetings in your office to talk with subordinates about operations and problems. Usually a small group of three to seven is large enough. You will be surprised how much you will learn just sitting around a table when everyone has his jacket off. Don't worry if you can't give them answers to some of the problems they bring up. Just by listening to them you make them feel that you are interested in them and their ideas. This also gives you a chance to watch potential leaders perform.

4. Develop the habit of getting bad news without overreacting. Grant your subordinates the right to make a mistake and don't lose your temper when they do. By doing this employees will level with you and you won't have "yes" men around you. If you react like a cannon when they goof or disagree with you, then you are coming down with executive isolation.

5. Invite letters or opinions from employees directly to you. These should be unsigned until subordinates know they can trust you. By doing this you may learn of problems that are small but growing such as a new organizational policy that is not popular. With this "safe" channel, despite a few crack-pot letters, you will find that when free expression is honestly asked for people will respond quickly and truthfully.

6. Conduct employee opinion surveys. These can be done cheaply by an outside communications expert and provide you with reliable information because such surveys provide the employee with the protection of anonymity. Often these complaints will tip you off to a deep-rooted problem among the rank and file. This survey type of information puts you in direct communication with subordinates because their replies come straight to you without being filtered by some well-meaning aide. Often you may not have as much time as you would like to talk with workers, but the survey if done properly can provide you with a form of person-to-person communication.

7. Recognize and reward any good idea that comes from a subordinate. This may be in the form of a letter or memo, money, or a special commendation. Such things will go a long way toward establishing a communication climate in your organization in which information bubbles to the top.

As a leader you do many things, make plans, solve problems, and motivate subordinates, but if you are out of touch with what's happening, your effectiveness as a leader will be severely impaired.

Measuring Your Leadership Style

If you are wondering where you fall in terms of leadership style, that is, are you more autocratic than democratic then answer the following questions. The results will indicate your overall leadership style via communication in three supervisory tasks. When you have finished, turn to page 113 and write down the number that corresponds with the space you checked in each area. Remember this leadership evaluation has no right or wrong answers so be honest. It simply measures the leadership style you most commonly use when dealing with your subordinates.

Instructions: Place a checkmark in front of the statement that you most agree with or most likely would do.

I. *Planning*

a. —————— I get my people together who have relevant information, so that we can review the whole problem and discuss ideas and strategies. Then we set up goals and objectives, schedules and ground rules—and establish individual responsibilities.

b. _____ After explaining the goals and objectives, I make individual work assignments for each subordinate. I tell each one that they can come and talk to me if they need help in carrying out their assignments.

c. _____ I do very little planning, either by myself or with my subordinates. I tell them what I want done and that I have confidence in them by telling them, "I'm sure you can and will do this job well."

d. _____ I give my people broad assignments and let them work out the details. I don't give them goals, objectives, or schedules. I let them do the planning.

e. _____ I do the planning by setting goals, objectives and work schedules that my people must follow. Then I work out the procedures and the ground rules each is to follow.

II. *Operations*

a. _____ I watch each of my subordinates closely and review their progress with them. If one of them has a problem or hits a snag, then I give him support.

b. _____ I tour the shop and watch my people, but I do very little on-the-spot action. I let people solve their own problems.

c. _____ I tour the shop to see if people are content and if they have the things they request.

d. _____ I stay on top with major points of progress and use my influence by identifying problems and changing strategies and work assignments with subordinates. I give them assistance when necessary by removing red tape and difficulties.

e. _____ I watch the work closely, criticize when necessary, and implement changes when necessary.

III. *Wrap Up*

a. _____ I make plans for the next assignment and move people to where they are needed. I give recognition and correct problems with individuals on a one-on-one basis.

b. _____ I conduct a final session to evaluate how the job went, good and bad, so that something can be learned from it. When appropriate, I give recognition for team effort as well as for outstanding individual contributions.

c. _____ I ask my superior what the next job is and assign people to do it.

d. _____ I hold a final meeting to congratulate the group as well as individuals. We discuss what did and did not work and what caused friction on the job. I try to reduce mistakes and resolve conflicts.

e. _____ I have a final meeting to go over the group's good points as well as mistakes and to show them ways in which they can improve. Then I give them the next job assignment, and each person gets the chance to discuss any reasonable suggestions he may have for improvement.

IV. *Overall Leadership Philosophy*

a. ———————— Be fair but firm. Use positive and negative incentives to get performance. Morale is as important as machines when it comes to producing at top efficiency.

b. ———————— The best way to get top performance is to set high standards and reward those individuals who meet them. Those who don't should be dealt with rather than ignored.

c. ———————— In the long run, it's best to maintain the work load at a comfortable tempo. Work for satisfaction and security among your employees.

d. ———————— Assign people tasks and leave them alone so they can do it.

e. ———————— Get effective production through participation and involvement of subordinates. Ask them for ideas. Understanding and cooperation are the keys to planning and managing.

Now check the grid below to interpret your answers.

This test is based on the Managerial Grid developed by industrial psychologists Robert R. Blake and Jane S. Mouton. They plot five major leadership styles, 1,1; 1,9; 9,1; 5,5; and 9,9. In their grid they measure these five styles along two axes: horizontal (concern for production) and vertical (concern for people). On the horizontal axis, 1 represents the lowest concern for production while 9 represents the highest. On the vertical axis, 1 represents the lowest concern for people and 9 represents the highest.

In identifying your leadership style, your selection of the first number reflects your concern for production, and the second number represents your concern for people. In looking at the five leadership styles plotted by Blake and Mouton, the autocrat— shown as 9,1—has the highest concern for production and the lowest for people. The missionary—shown as 1,9—has the highest concern for people, but the lowest for production. The deserter— shown as 1,1—reflects a leader that has little concern for production or people. The executive—shown as 9,9—represents a leader with the highest concern for production and people. The compromiser—shown as 5,5—reflects a leader who has a healthy concern for production and people.What was your leadership style in each of the four tasks? Translate your answers into these styles.

Planning	Operations	Wrap Up	Overall Leadership Philosophy
a. 9,9	a. 5,5	a. 9,1	a. 5,5
b. 5,5	b. 1,1	b. 9,9	b. 9,1
c. 1,9	c. 1,9	c. 1,1	c. 1,9
d. 1,1	d. 9,9	d. 1,9	d. 1,1
e. 9,1	e. 9,1	e. 5,5	e. 9,9

After measuring your leadership style, remember that there is no single style naturally more effective than others. Effectiveness depends on a style being appropriate to the situation in which it is used. It appears then that since situations vary, so must the leader's style. Sometimes he must be production-oriented and other times people-oriented. Research findings and common sense support this conclusion.

The leadership style evaluation you've just taken gives you some idea of what type of style you usually use when interacting (communicating) with your subordinates. The evaluation gives you this picture of yourself, but it also underscores that leadership must aim for style flexibility rather than style rigidity. Styles are best seen in relation to specific situations. Any style has a situation appropriate to it, and many situations that are inappropriate. The formula for effective leadership at the beginning of the chapter illustrates this.

As you look over your selections again you find your basic *dominant* leadership style. This is the one you use most often. If you look closely you should see your *back-up* style. This is the one you use most often after your dominant style. Finally, if you analyze your scores closely, you should find your *rejected* style. This is the leadership style you rarely use. Study this one closely because an unwillingness or inability to use this style when the situation demands it leads to a loss of effectiveness.

In the future when you find yourself in a leadership role and you are considering how to behave toward others, remember the formula for effective leadership: leadership is a function of personality traits, the situation at hand, and the resulting style when communicating with others.

8

DECISION MAKING: MORE THAN FACTS ARE NEEDED

Life always gets harder toward the summit—the cold increases, responsibility increases.

Nietzsche

If you ask someone in authority, "What do you need to make a decision?" he will usually ask you, "What information is available?"

Probably no single behavior reflects a manager's role better than the task of decision making. H. A. Simon says that "decision making is synonymous with management."

While the quality of the decision depends on the quality of the information available, decision making is a lot more than the mere sifting of facts. You have probably noticed that the higher you go in your organization and the more responsibility you assume, the more your decisions are based on such nonfactual elements as hunches, experience, practicalities, and personality.

What you may have noticed is that there are never enough hard cold facts to determine which is the best choice. There is never enough evidence to make your selection easy. If you had all the facts you needed to make a choice you wouldn't be making a decision, because decision making is the selection of alternatives. You make your choice on the basis of incomplete information. According to Peter Drucker, a decision is judgment or a choice between alternatives. Thus you can never hope to have all the facts when faced with a decision, so you exercise judgment.

In today's organization decision making must be viewed as something a lot more complex than choosing between alternatives.

115

The decision-making process relies on planning, setting goals and objectives as well as behaviors that lead to decisions, and the implementation of them, such as information flows, perception, and feedback. In a sense, decision making has two principal activities: the actual decision-making process and a decision-making strategy.

THE DECISION-MAKING PROCESS

When considering the decision-making process, one is essentially talking about a list of steps that should be followed. For example:

1. Define problem.
2. Develop decision criteria.
3. Generate alternatives.
4. Measure outcomes.
5. Make decision.

The first thing the decision maker must do is to properly define the problem he is facing. If the problem isn't defined properly, then you may be working on the wrong problem or the wrong part of the right problem. Drucker offers some help here as he distinguishes between problems that are unique (exceptional cases) and those that are generic (processed according to rules that are applicable to all problems of this nature). According to Drucker, the effective decision maker always begins by assuming that the problem is generic; that it can be handled by established rules or procedures. That is, the problem is similar to a previous problem that was handled successfully. Often the decision maker finds that the problem can't be handled by established rules and he must search for new procedures. Actually most organizational problems require some combination of rules and new ways for solving them.

Most of the exceptional decision makers I've known have the ability to tell the difference between a problem that can be handled by routine procedures and one that will require some unique methods of dealing with it. The trick is how to do this.

Generally decision makers use their time and energy to clearly define the problem at hand, rather than searching for an answer. They do this by asking a series of questions. Is it really a problem or could it be a symptom? Is the problem in my area of responsibility? Can I realistically do anything about it? What will happen if I do nothing? Will time cure it? If I solve it will it create new problems in other areas?

Answers to these questions provide the effective decision maker with some idea if the problem (if it is actually one) is generic or unique. Once this is established the decision maker can go on to the other steps in the decision-making process.

In my consulting work I have found decision makers have the most trouble identifying the actual problem rather than the symptom. Too many people jump to the conclusion that they have identified a problem if they find a situation that seems to be having some negative effect on their department. It is usually helpful to them to point out that the cure for a disease is not always found at the site of the epidemic. They should stop and discover the cause of this negative effect. Having done this they will have identified the real problem.

TYPES OF DECISIONS

Basically there are two types of decision categories in an organization, routine and risk.

Most experts estimate that about 90 percent of the decisions made in an organization are of the routine variety. Routine decisions are the everyday, repetitive decisions such as bookkeeping tasks, traditional forms that must be filled out, and ordering supplies. Viewed individually such decisions really don't have that much impact on the total organization, but if you lump them all together they may spell success or failure for the organization. Generally routine decisions are made in the lower ranks of the organization. A line supervisor may make many such decisions, but the head of an organization would make very few. Usually routine decisions are made according to tradition, rules, or time-honored procedures.

Decisions involving risk are basic to the survival of the organization. Usually they involve long range commitments of resources, human and financial, and affect the very welfare of the organization. Such decisions involving risk fall somewhere on a continuum between "certainty" and "uncertainty." In reality it is difficult to think of any decision that is "certain." However, for the purpose of this discussion the label will be used to describe a decision that involves much experience and high predictability of certain outcomes. It is different from a routine decision because more risk is involved. For example, a car dealer may order x number of cars for his showroom when the new models come out. There is the risk that he may order too many or too few. However, based on his thirty years' experience as a new-car dealer we would feel confident that he can predict how many cars he will sell for a given time period.

At the other end of the continuum, a completely "uncertain" decision is one for which there is little if any experience and little prediction of the outcomes. Here the decision maker is on his own and has little knowledge of what outcomes will result from his decision. Some of the earlier NASA space missions represent this type of situation. As problems arose in space, Mission Control in Houston had to make decisions based on high levels of uncertainty. Most middle- and upper-management decisions are of the risk type.

COMMUNICATION AND THE DECISION PROCESS

Communication affects every phase of the decision-making process, but in particular it serves two functions. It provides information to base the decisions on, and it persuades people to follow the decision once it has been made.

In terms of the communication activity inside the head of the decision maker, Herbert A. Simon has outlined three major phases in the decision-making process. These are:

1. Intelligence activity. Here the decision maker surveys the organizational environment for problems that need to be decided.
2. Design activity. In this second phase the decision maker develops and analyzes possible courses of action to take.
3. Choice activity. The third and final phase for the decision maker is to select a particular course of action.

These phases become more meaningful for the decision maker in an organization when they are put into a time sequence. For any problem that must be decided there is a past in which the problem developed, information builds up, and the need for a decision is recognized by someone in authority. Second, there is a present in which alternatives are generated and the final choice is made. Finally, there is the future in which the decision is implemented and the eventual feedback detailing its success or failure. What is apparent here is that decision making should be viewed from a process perspective. This means that decision making is not the single act of choosing alternative A over alternative B, but that the decision has a time sequence to it and is actually composed of a series of related steps.

Karl Weick offers the decision maker some interesting ideas when processing information related to a problem. Weick argues that an organization (composed of human decision makers) has two means of dealing with information. It can determine the worth of a piece of information by employing *rules* to analyze it, or it can pass the information through a number of *cycles* (people actually look at it trying to decide under what rule it fits).

An organizational example is the clerk who replies to a customer complaint by the use of Form Letter 1-A. Here she has selected a rule (a standard form letter)—made her decision on how to deal with the problem based on a rule. But suppose the complaint was of a unique nature. She decides that of her ten form letters none are appropriate. She then passes it on to her supervisor thus generating a new cycle for dealing with the problem (information).

Borrowing from Weick several options are now evident for the decision maker in an organization. If you are able to establish more rules for handling information (problems) then you and your staff will be engaged in fewer cycles thus saving time and energy. In a sense, you are trying to turn the problem into a routine one covered by procedures. The more rules you have the fewer the cycles.

However, the rub is that your rules may not be appropriate to the problem (information) at hand. Therefore, you must go through more cycles in order to deal with this unique problem. In short, the fewer the rules the more cycles you have.

For the decision maker the implementation is clear; save most of your time and energy for those unique problems requiring more cycles. Have your staff handle as many problems as they can by the use of procedures and rules. This gives you more time for thinking about the decisions involving risk.

DECISION-MAKING BEHAVIOR

Method of Solving Problem

		known	unknown
Type of Problem	routine	I Recurring type of problem. Solve by rules and procedures.	II Problem has occurred before. Solve by cycles and unique methods.
	risk	III Unique problem. Methods for solving it are calculated.	IV Unique problem. Methods for solving it are uncalculable.

In Cell I the decision maker is in good shape. He can identify the problem as recurring or routine. Methods for handling this type of problem have been worked out and are simply put into effect when this type of problem occurs.

In Cell II the decision maker has more difficulty. He has seen this type of problem before, but because it has some unique aspects to it the exact method (alternatives) for solving it are unknown. That is, specific alternatives must be worked out based not on rules and procedures as much as on judgment, past experience, and consensus. Because of this the decision maker is not sure what outcomes will result from his decision.

In Cell III the decision maker faces real difficulties. The problem is unique. He must concentrate on clearly defining the problem. Once this is done he can select from some known alternatives for solving it. For example, if an automobile won't start a mechanic may not know why, but he has a set of things (alternatives) that he can do to start the car providing the problem is minor.

In Cell IV the decision maker is in his greatest difficulty. He is faced with all the difficulties of Cell III plus no known methods for solving the problem. The problem must be defined and a method of solving it has to be generated. These acts will require major energy and skill on his part.

Obviously in any organization an effective decision maker attempts to move all of his decisions toward Cell I. If he can move the decision to Cell I, he reduces most if not all the risk from his decision.

However, while such an effort should be the decision maker's goal it is not without danger. The decision maker must be aware of the temptation to make certain assumptions ("That problem is just like the one we had last year in Dallas") so that he can operate within the safety of Cell I. In short, he must resist the temptation to define the problem so that it fits some existing procedures for handling it. He must resist the temptation to "follow the book on this one." In the short run this may keep his superior off his back, but in the long run the problem may blow up in his face. He must not force the problem into Cell I when it is actually a Cell III problem.

"FACTS"—NO PERFECT ANSWER

So many decision makers when confronted with a problem search frantically for that one piece of information or fact that will solve their difficulty. They look for the perfect answer assuming that it is buried in some stack of information. They keep asking for more information rather than deciding on an alternative and working to implement it. Soon they are suffering from information overload with the usual displaying of anxiety and indecision. The collection of more and more information will at some point be counterproductive to effective decision making with the more relevant and most important facts hopelessly buried under the weight of the collected data. Precious time is lost as the decision maker must sift the facts "hoping to get on top of the situation."

George Ball points out that "time relentlessly destroys unexercised options." For the decision maker the message is clear: avoid getting mired in a mass of petty detail.

PERCEPTIONS AND DECISION MAKING

While an organization is influenced by events from outside its walls, it is largely controlled by central decision makers. While decisions may be based on collected "facts" in reality what actually happens is that a decision maker's perceptions—his definition of the facts or situation—rather than objective facts influence the subsequent decision that is made.

As a decision maker confronted with a number of possible choices, one may ask, "What determines which choice you make?" A large portion of the answer is your beliefs about the facts or information in the situation. This means that we construct the reality in which we operate. We take our perception of the world as objective reality, not realizing that our view of reality is very subjective. We know the report from a rival firm is no good because we've seen it; we know our enemy in a committee meeting is trying to impress the boss because we can hear what he is saying; we know the new division chief is hostile because we have seen the actions he has taken. We know what is real.

However, we do not stop to consider that in fact the report may be good, your enemy may not be trying to impress the boss, and the new division chief may not be hostile. In fact our perceptions allow us to infer reality—a very subjective one, but one we feel very secure about. It is precisely in this feeling of certainty that the danger for the decision maker lies.

When a problem occurs requiring a decision, it may be legitimately perceived in several different ways. As a rule decision makers are going to view it so that it does not contradict their usual perceptions. In short, they are going to make it square with their other beliefs. In other words the decision maker may view the facts of the problem correctly, that is, he can objectively construct what has happened. But his interpretation of factual record may contain a perceptual error. Because of this it is crucial that a decision maker have some independent way to check his perceptions against reality.

For example, a manager that tends to view all labor complaints as attempts to avoid work can make some serious errors when deciding what to do. Because his perception of labor demands is always negative, he can't recognize a legitimate complaint about dangerous working conditions.

This means that our perceptions of an event are important because they influence the choices we will make in our decision. While it may seem abstract this means that we never respond to the actual problem, but to our view of it. The actual motivations of a rival in the organization does not determine your behavior, but your perception of his motives will cause you to act accordingly. This means that if you define a situation as real, it will be real in its consequences.

For these psychological reasons it is pure folly for a decision maker to say that he will let the objective facts make his decision for him. Facts must be collected, sifted, kept or rejected, ranked in order of importance, evaluated, and weighed. And all of these processes take place in one's mind and are thereby pushed, pulled, and shaped by one's emotions and perceptions. In fact in the collecting of facts or information much of what gets selected is subject to our perceptions. Social science research has repeatedly shown that a person selectively exposes himself to information that is consistent with his beliefs. Because our beliefs are stable and we resist changing them a decision maker confronted with two alternatives, A and B, will most likely choose the one that preserves his beliefs. Thus a personal bias may keep some crucial information from being collected or passed up to a decision maker. This natural process of selection is always present and a decision maker must take safeguards against it.

In summary, a decision maker's reality depends on two interlocked subjective processes: an information- or fact-gathering process that reflects the personal bias of the data gatherer; and the perception process that determines how the information or facts are to be interpreted.

PERCEPTION AND COMMUNICATION

In an organization information nearly always comes from below, and the more important it is, the farther down one has to go to gather it. Typically a decision maker will ask his secretary how much was spent on the department brochures last year. If she is not sure, she asks another secretary or clerk. Finally the information is collected and passed back up the chain of command. Because the person that ultimately supplies the information doesn't realize that this is a high level request he may not gather the facts carefully. The result is that the decision maker bases his important decision on figures that may well be wrong.

If we extend this idea on information flow to the entire organization, it is obvious that the channels of communication on which the organization's perception depends is made up of chains of individuals. The individuals, as in our previous example, are not mere photocopying machines that passively relay the information on to the next person. Each is an individual with personal perceptions and each will decide what to report up the chain. The decision maker must realize that his flow of information travels through a chain of communication and this consists of a series of decisions by individuals. Thus the organization's perception is shaped by the perceptions of each of these individuals.

Snyder and Paige have formulated several laws that govern an organization's "perceptual" process.

1. The less information about external events, the more reliance on information within the unit making the policy decision.
2. The more limited the information, the greater the emphasis on the reliability of the source.
3. The greater the confidence in the existing information, the more contrary information will be needed to change the current interpretation.
4. The more routine the times, the more information must have crisislike qualities if it is to gain top-level attention.

Thus when considering alternatives, the wise decision maker will evaluate his information based on these four laws. In addition, he should consider the amount of information used compared to the amount actually available; the amount used relative to the amount needed; the reliability of the information; and the degree of confidence in the interpretations made on the basis of the information.

For example, let's consider a crisis in an organization; the union employees have walked off their jobs. In the beginning of the week the organization's top executives used only a small portion of the total amount of information available. This condition would likely continue until about midweek when the amount used would exceed the amount needed with many small bits of information from many sources flowing into the executive offices. In the beginning of the decision week the reliability of the information was rated low, but by midweek the interpretation of most of the information was higher than it ever had been. Why is this?

Probably the personal perceptions of the executives have taken over, and they have begun to fit the incoming information into mental pigeonholes. What has happened is evident. An executive would form his opinion on which choices should be made on the basis of little information. Once he had done this it became impossible to change it because it governed (selective perception) his perception of future information.

Another factor affecting the quality of information flowing to a decision maker is the fact that communication is often rewarded or punished. This helps to explain why the organization's communication system is biased by the ideas and plans (likes and dislikes) of the top executives. A subordinate is rewarded if he passes up information that interests his boss. However, if he passes up information that his superior feels is unimportant or displeases him, it is likely to cost him. As a result a subordinate soon learns what information to pass up to his superior. If a subordinate is forced to present a report that he knows will displease his superior, he may likely water down the report so that it is more acceptable. The error may then be compounded because the superior may not carefully read the report and miss some of the negative information contained in it. Subordinates soon get skillful at passing up information in "raw" form, i. e., just "facts" because they know these can be interpreted in any way.

In general, despite the powerful influences of our perceptions on information, most decision makers still believe that the truth or correct choice will be obvious when all the facts are presented.

Our knowledge of such processes may offer some remedies. An individual decision maker can increase the accuracy of his perceptions by establishing a procedure that forces him to question his own beliefs. For example, if an organization is considering moving into a new market area it often hires consultants or instructs its own personnel to gather facts that would support investing resources in this new area. This is part of the marketing picture, but it should also hire or instruct others to make a case against going into this new market. Now the decision maker would have two sets of facts before making the final choice. The individual decision maker should ask someone in his group to look for information that goes against the favored choice and to collect this information so that it is passed upward rather than filtered out. If this is not done the various people in the chain of communication may selectively filter out contrary information.

For example, in a large research and development firm when the request for a proposal came in, various executives at different levels would examine it in order to decide whether to go for the contract. Subordinates were quick to catch the way the wind was blowing—particularly if the implicit decision was to go for it—and prepare reports and other pieces of information as to why the organization should bid on the contract. Dissonant facts would occasionally emerge, but such bits of information generally lack the strength to have much effect on the decision-making process. The evidence would be rejected in various chains of command before it could be collected into a convincing negative case.

What was needed in this case was a formal group or report that could build a strong case—strong enough to compete with the powerful psychological forces that are saying, "Yes we should bid on this project."

Such a group within the office or department should:

1. Look for information contrary to the popular case.
2. Collect such negative information.
3. Provide feedback and be sure that unpopular ideas or views are heard at high levels.
4. Make a reasonable case for the alternate position.

DECIDING WHAT TO DECIDE ABOUT

In an organization or the world of action a decision maker rarely has enough time to explore all the parts of a problem before he must make some choices for dealing with it. In short, he must select alternatives under a time constraint. Therefore, he must allocate his time between serious matters for which a decision is required. He must make a decision before he ever gets to the problem at hand—how he will use his decision-making time. He must decide which problems can wait awhile. Then for those remaining problems he must decide which ones are top priority. Through this time devoted to deciding what to decide about he has actually decided how he will allocate the remainder of his decision-making time.

To do this a decision maker should analyze or survey the range of issues before him and see if any of them have to do with current operations. If performance is not up to par then actions must be taken to correct this. Here the time constraint is so powerful that this type of problem, affecting current operations, must be dealt with first.

Then the decision maker, having solved current problems or found none in the issues before him, may turn to future problems or opportunities. Such issues generally have to do with planning with the focus on the future. Here the decisions should be ranked according to gain. Gain can be anything such as profits, morale, productivity, service, and learning. Decisions having the greater likely gain should be made before those having lesser gain. In short, the decision maker is looking for an opportunity for making improvements.

How one will measure "gain" is not simple or always clear, but this is what decision making is all about. Issues that require decisions will vary from organization to organization and with the problems themselves so there is no single definition of gain that will apply to every decision. With some problems, such as dividends due to interest rates, a fairly clear measure of what is a gain is apparent, but other problems like increasing employee morale will be less precise. This is where the decision maker's judgment comes into play. The point is not to look for a single unit of gain that can be applied to every problem, but for the decision maker to use this concept when ranking the issues for decision analysis.

This notion of gain can be used to help cure a common disease of decision makers—indecision. When faced with a tough complex decision, many have a tendency to do nothing. If this happens to you (and it touches all of us at some point in our careers) try moving yourself off of dead center by estimating the gain obtained from action in the situation as compared to the outcome expected without action (no decision).

When someone chooses not to make a decision or postpones a decision, he is actually choosing to do nothing. What the person doesn't realize is that he has actually made a decision with consequences perhaps as risky as any of the possible alternatives he didn't select. Because of this indecision, he may find that he has less rather than more freedom to operate. Over time such refusals to take action become events that will eventually force him to take action—make a decision that he may not want to make. In short, circumstances will sooner or later force him to make a decision.

While power may corrupt, someone has to lead. As President Carter has said: "Someone's got to make difficult decisions. It is the responsibility of an elected official to exercise his options while he can, not try to preserve them."

DECISION MAKING IN A CRISIS

There is only one rule for making decisions in a crisis—don't ever get trapped this way again. Any effective decision maker is not going to get "his back against the wall." Any sudden difficulty is not a crisis. If it is a true crisis then it has been long in the making, usually resulting from months or years without meeting the problem head on and solving it.

Most decision makers have one problem in common—they have too many problems to handle. You may feel that you are not getting anywhere, that you are caught on a treadmill in which you have to make too many decisions too quickly. In effect, you have spread yourself too thin and you end up doing many things but none of them well. Of even more importance you don't have any time for looking ahead for the opportunities that are out there for you and your organization. You don't have time to plan because you are overtaken by daily events. There is a preoccupation with recurring problems and you have no time to solve them with a view to shaping the future.

A solution for getting out of this vicious circle is to employ H. Ford Dickie's rule. He advises you to list all of the decisions you must make in order of importance. Then select the top 20 percent as the critical few and identify the remaining 80 percent as the trivial many. Now spend most of your time and energy on the critical few. The 20/80 percent has shown on the average that 80 percent of the results in a situation can be attributed to 20 percent of the possible choices. This rule will help you reverse the trend toward dilution of effort and getting caught in the crisis trap.

Ralph E. Lewis has developed a percentage breakdown of the amount of time various levels of decision makers should spend on organizational problems. He argues there are two types of decisions—reviewing past performance and action on future events. He calls for:

1. For higher management, spend 20 percent of your time on the first category (reviewing past performance) and give the remaining 80 percent of your available time to the second category (planning for the future).
2. For middle management, split your available time on a 50–50 basis between the two categories.
3. For lower management, do not spend more than 80 percent of your time on the first category and give the remaining 20 percent of your available time to category two.

The point is obvious: by reducing the amount of time you spend in reviewing past performance and filling out reports (delegate much of this work to subordinates), you will have more time for solving problems and planning for future opportunities. You want your decision making to force you to be oriented toward the future.

Creativity in Decision Making

In today's organization creativity is a necessary part of effective decision making. While this sounds simple enough, most decision makers have no idea of how to achieve it. Creativity means to make something new—nearly always out of reshaping existing materials. This is an important point to remember because it doesn't mean you have to start from scratch in your decision making, but you begin with what you have whether it is existing materials or procedures for doing things.

Social science research offers considerable help in bringing creativity to your decision making. Graham Wallas has identified four basic steps in the creative process: preparation, incubation, illumination, and verification. In other words, a creative decision proceeds through certain orderly stages of development.

In the preparation stage you realize that a decision is needed and you prepare for it by gathering information. You study the problem at hand identifying all the aspects of it. Your goal is to see all sides of it and run through them freely in your mind so that you have complete understanding of the issue.

Often in the preparation stage no solution to the problem is discovered so the decision process moves to the incubation stage. Here you simply shelve the problem and forget about it for awhile. Anxiety and frustration often build in the preparation stage and at some point if this reaches too high a level, it is best to walk away from the problem and let your mind cool. It is somewhat analogous to a computer that has an overload switch—it automatically shuts itself off when it has too much information or a program won't run rather than blowing its circuits.

This doesn't mean you completely forget about the problem. You will think about it from time to time, but never for too long.

In the illumination stage you should get a sudden insight or a spontaneous solution to the problem. The light bulb turns on, and the idea that has been incubating takes shape. The history of inventions is full of such sudden solutions. Many top executives say they get their insights into a tough problem while shaving.

Verification is the final step in creative decision making. The bright idea you had in the illumination stage must be translated, verified, revised, and made into something useful. The manager must debug his marketing plan and the new service plan must actually be made to work.

The creative process is crucial to the effective decision maker as today's organizations face new problems and different environments in which past solutions may be inappropriate.

PSYCHOLOGICAL BARRIERS TO DECISION MAKING

As organizations move into a more complex age, decision makers are going to have to recognize and overcome psychological barriers to the decision process.

As pointed out earlier, the decision maker needs more than just facts, because the decision process is influenced directly by many psychological factors. The decision maker is influenced by his personality, group pressure, the organizational climate, communication processes, and a whole group of psychological and social variables. Many of these psychological factors act as filters or blockades in the decision process.

Katz and Kahn have identified seven psychological principles that often undermine rational decision making. They are:

1. Determination of thought by position in social space. This means that a person's thoughts are influenced by his surrounding environment—culture, organization, or department. For example, a decision maker surrounded by yes men is not going to get dissenting information from his subordinates.
2. Identification with outside reference groups. Here the decision maker identifies with prestigious groups outside the organization. This could be a prestigious competitor, professional association, or highly paid consultants.
3. Projection of attitudes and values. Decision makers often make the false assumption that other groups share the same values they do.
4. Global or undifferentiated thinking. There is a tendency for decision makers to oversimplify or fail to recognize differences in the problems facing them. "All unions are the same."
5. Dichotomized thinking. Here the decision maker either refuses to or can't see gray areas to the problem. Everything is viewed as yes/no or black/white. In the real world this is dangerous.
6. Cognitive nearsightedness. In this situation the decision maker only responds to the immediate and the obvious. Here the short run is

considered more important and the implications for the long run are ignored. This type of decision maker is more interested in being a fireman and putting out daily fires than thinking about problems and future considerations rationally.

7. Oversimplified notions of causation. This means the decision maker is quick to find the cause of the problem—in fact, too quick. Most of the time this type of decision maker identifies the symptom, rather than the cause. He has never learned that causation is complex and should not be oversimplified.

TRICKS FOR AVOIDING DECISIONS

In my own consulting and organizational work experience, I conclude the most dangerous person in an organization is someone, charged with responsibility, who won't make decisions. The effects of such indecisiveness are overwhelming. An organization will drift, flounder, or fail when an executive can't make up his mind. Top personnel who seriously want to make the organization number one will become frustrated because needed decisions aren't forthcoming and will leave. As a result the organization is left without highly motivated people, a key ingredient for organizational effectiveness.

In addition, a poor decision is better than no decision in many cases because other people can use energy, skills, and ideas to make it work. With no decision employees can do nothing.

STRATEGIES

Managers who won't make decisions employ a number of strategies. Here are some strategies you are sure to recognize.

1. Collect more information. "We don't have all the facts yet," seems to be a favorite phrase of the indecisive. While having the facts is an important consideration, most likely this strategy is a trick for avoiding a decision.

2. Equate new problems with old ones. Here the indecisive is saying, "We've always handled problems like that this way and it's worked." Past experience is an adequate guideline if you can forget that time changes things such as new competition, a shrinking market, new laws, technological progress, economic conditions, politics, and hundreds of other things. It must be remembered that not every problem is similar to one that occurred in the past.

3. The timing is wrong. This could be correct, but it probably is a ploy to do nothing and let time run out by purposely missing a deadline.

4. Appoint a committee to study it. Faced with a tricky problem that needs an immediate decision, the indecisive sets up a committee to study it and report back to him. Committees can and do, do important work, but they can also be used as an excuse for avoiding

a decision. What will probably happen is that the problem will likely be forgotten before the committee reports back.

5. Create a crisis. Rather than make a hard black and white choice, the indecisive will find a "crisis" to take his mind and others off the immediate problem. Often he will say, "I know we have to deal with that problem, but this latest thing has to be dealt with first." He thereby sidesteps a decision.

6. Hire an expert. Here the indecisive is using a fairly sophisticated technique to get out of making a decision. Usually he can be heard to say, "This is just too technical for us, or outside our area of expertise." After the expert (a consultant) gives his advice the indecisive will hide behind his report for making a decision, or he will use the expert's advice in order not to make a decision by saying, "We had better hold off on this; even the experts can't agree."

As a consultant I've been asked to do such hand holding along with making a decision for some manager. When told, "You're the expert, tell me what I should do," I point out that is not my role as a consultant. My job is to gather information, evaluate it, and make recommendations—but not decisions. Managers are paid to do that.

7. See which way the wind is blowing. This is a subtle way of avoiding thinking through a problem and making a decision. Here the indecisive tries to determine what higher-ups are thinking and decide accordingly. This is organizational politics and not courageous decision making and it can doom a plan as quickly as any of the other strategies for avoiding a decision.

Steps for Effective Decision Making

Peter Drucker says that decision makers don't make their most serious mistakes because they select wrong alternatives, but because they try to answer wrong questions. So your first step for effective decision making is to:

1. Identify your goal. Analyze what it is you are after, where it is you want to be, or what you want to happen.

2. Develop your objectives. Here you are putting your goal(s) into action by nailing down some specific behaviors. You determine this by asking "how" for each goal and then when you get an answer as to what you should do, you ask how again.

Remember that facts and emotions go into decision making, so realize that the decision process is more than collecting facts.

3. Weigh the choices. Compare the risks of each course of action against the desired result (your goal). Face the fact that your choice may be the wrong one and you'll have to live with it. Remember, however, there are no riskless decisions or even riskless nonaction—but there is a need for you to decide on some course of action.

4. Estimate your lead time. Determine the amount of time you have to make a decision with the urgency of the need for results. If you find yourself in a situation that is crucial to your organization's operations—then you may have to make a quick decision. If you are in a situation that calls for a decision that will affect the future of the organization for a long time, then you may want to take your time and consider each alternative carefully before deciding on a course of action.

5. Decide. Whatever alternative you finally select, you've grown considerably as a decision maker if you've learned there are no easy answers to difficult problems. If you have asked the right questions chances are the right answers will appear. In the final analysis, it's a matter of being true to yourself. You can't let fear of the unknown paralyze you into doing nothing—remember the right decision won't automatically fall on your desk, you have to make it happen.

Are You a Good Decision Maker?

Take a look at your decision-making habits. Ask yourself:

1. Do you seek out problems rather than waiting for them to land on your desk?
2. Do you set priorities when addressing problems?
3. Do you make time for analyzing the long range effects of your decisions?
4. Do you review organizational policy to see if it's still applicable to today's problems?
5. Do you make your own decisions or constantly seek the advice of others?
6. Do you know when a problem needs a quick decision?
7. Do you decide or let problems take care of themselves?

An answer of "no" to any of these questions means that you could be more effective in your decision making.

Types of Decisions

In the organization decisions boil down to binary choices, "go" or "no go," at some point in the decision process. At some point the buck will stop on someone's desk—ultimately it may be yours. By "go" or "no go," coming from the NASA era, one simply means that a decision maker must decide to do something or decide not to. Essentially the decision finally becomes for someone a clear black or white choice—a yes or no type of action. Do we implement the new plan? Do we buy more equipment? Do we invest heavily in the new market? Do we scrap a plan that isn't working well? Do we fire Joe?

Two results are possible for each go or no go decision.

A go decision that works. Suppose you decide to enter a new territory with your sales personnel and as a result you increase your sales by 15 percent. Here your go decision turned out right because it worked.

A go decision that fails. You decide to hire a new personnel director and as a result employees are unhappy, turnover increases, productivity falls, and morale sags. You've made a go decision—a positive action—but it has failed.

A no go decision that works. You decide not to buy new equipment, counting on the old equipment to last another year with minimum repairs. At the end of the year you've had few repairs so here you've made a no go decision that worked.

A no go decision that fails. You decide not to promote Ed to division chief and, as a result, he leaves the organization. You've lost a valuable subordinate through your no go decision that failed.

In my observation, decision makers are more reluctant to make go decisions. They prefer to make no go ones. Why? Because the go decision places the decision maker in the spotlight. By making the go decision he assumes the responsibility for its working.

Although the go decision is the best one in that it offers the greatest rewards, most decision makers prefer to make no go ones because failures here are difficult to pin on anyone.

For example, if a decision maker decides to buy a failing company hoping to turn it around, the company had better end up in the black. He has clearly accepted responsibility for his go decision. If the decision fails this can follow him the rest of his career. However, had he made a no go decision and decided not to buy the company and even though later it is evident he should have he can exercise several options to lessen the error. He can be blunt and say, "I learned my lesson on that one, and I won't ever make that mistake again." He has created the image that when the opportunity comes along again he will seize it. Second, he can say he was for the acquisition all along, but others wouldn't go for it. If believed, he will have successfully shifted some of the blame to others.

In an organization's memory usually only go decisions are remembered so the decision maker had better be right on them. If they work, you are applauded, but if they fail, you are in trouble. This explains much of the timid behavior of most decision makers and starts them drifting to the indecisive.

ESP and Decision Making

As noted earlier, as you rise in the organization your decisions are based less on facts (because they aren't available) and more on judgment and hunches. Often such decisions have to do with future events—what you predict will happen; and unfortunately data aren't available on what is likely to happen down the road in most cases.

Perhaps there is another factor that can help you in this situation. Research done at the New Jersey Institute of Technology under John Mihalasky strongly suggests that some decision makers have more ability to predict future events than others. Because of this extrasensory perception (ESP), when decision makers are operating in situations where information isn't available, they are able to make better decisions.

Using a test for measuring an executive's ESP, the research indicates that superior profit makers tend to be better guessers or hunch players.

The superior group was also found tending to do better because they do *not* make decisions under stress or anxiety unless necessary. In their offices they are better able to evoke this ESP ability when they have an intense emotional tie to the problem, but then step back, relax, and let the subconscious take over.

Apparently many superior decision makers have this ESP ability and are better able to play their hunches as well as deciding by logic and rationality.

Today some organizations make candidates for promotion take precognition tests. And because research has shown that executives tend to make their best decisions while not under stress and anxiety, concerning problems with which they have had a deep emotional tie, several major corporations have provided executives with areas where they can relax.

Mihalasky suggests on the basis of his ESP research that if you want to improve your decision-making ability try this: Make your hard decisions when you are relaxed and free from anxiety. Get deeply involved with the problem through the collection of information and talking with people—become more than casually involved. Don't laugh; learn that hunches can be crucial to your effectiveness as a decision maker. Keep a record of when you use your intuitive guesses (ESP) and how the decisions turn out.

COMPUTERIZED DECISION MAKING

Computers can't replace people in the organization's decision process. The machines can be tremendous tools for management, but as decision makers they've been oversold.

One of the great myths of the organizational world has been that eventually all decisions will be made by computer. For years the talk has been that the entire organization's information flow would turn into one big "on line system," with a constant flow of information ending in a printout of daily decisions. Corporate history details a different reality. Lockheed Aircraft, using a computerized management control system for decision making, managed to overrun its C5A transport plane budget by $2 billion, and would have folded had it not been for a federal government rescue.

The conclusion is for you to take the computer out of your decision-making process. Contrary to the myth, computers are not magic tools. The hard reality is that the information they produce is only as good as what *someone* put in. A human being full of bias and the ability to make mistakes determines in the final analysis what the machine turns out.

But even more importantly, another human being determines what use to make of the data that are spewed out. No single person, or even a staff of people, has the time or the ability to analyze and understand the tons that a computer can produce overnight. As a decision maker you often have to make quick decisions, and you can't wait for a lengthy analysis of a computer readout. In short, any information produced by the computer needs interpretation, and this usually requires a lot of manpower. Whatever question you ask, the electronic wizard, if it is in a good mood, will provide you with several answers, none of them in quite the form you need for a clear answer. And remember there is a crucial detail missing from your printout answer—what facts were programmed into the computer on which this answer is based.

A basic problem with the computer too involved in your decision process is that it will generate information that you really don't need. Everyone has experienced stacks of printouts on his desk that look impressive, but can't really be used for critical decision making. If you have a problem, you usually get the answers from people, not by flipping through a stack of printouts.

The computer has made the decision process easier by functioning as millions of adding machines and filing cabinets, and for storing messages. Someday it will graduate from being an overpaid bookkeeper to meaningful duties, but it will never replace the decision maker's need to think and exercise human judgment.

GETTING THEM TO DECIDE

Finally a closing word on getting others to decide. Briefly the thinking shifts here from your decision-making processes to focus on the decision of those you want to influence.

Communicating to another person exactly what you want him to do may tip your hand, or he may interpret your message as an ultimatum and therefore turn your request down.

The best communication rule, although it involves costs and risks, is to present your request in the form of a simple decision to the person you are trying to influence. This is true for two reasons. The more work you do in preparing the result you want to happen, the less work there is for another to do and the more likely he is to see things your way. Because you have built a solid case, based on hard work and information, he will have to work equally hard to tear it down. But by accepting your argument the second person has a far simpler task.

For a complex problem in which you need a decision whether it is yes or no the strategy is to get others to make a decision. Here what you need is a decision, not a maybe. It is not enough to present others with a problem and suggest that something should be done. They are likely to agree, but no decision will be made. A better communication strategy is to present others with something they can say yes or no to. For example, present them with a memorandum which makes a particular proposal and ends: yes _____;
no _____. This is far more likely to produce a decision.

Decision making is far more than just collecting facts. Facts or information are based on the subjective realities or perceptions of people in the decision chain. Hence, the decision-making process becomes a communication process, full of all the complexities that human beings generate.

9

BARRIERS AND BRIDGES TO COMMUNICATING WITH MINORITIES

All too often the man who says he has a communication problem may be the communication problem.

Antony Jay

For years many used the "melting pot" concept to characterize American society, but it has proven to be misleading and inadequate. Cultural differences do not melt, nor do they disappear; rather the cultural traits, customs, and mores are modified as they are passed from generation to generation. American society thus is not one massive homogeneous body of people; but it is a pluralistic society in which members of various cultural groups retain their identity, values, and traditions. Although these differences make us a distinctive and accomplished nation, they also contribute to communication breakdowns and failures.

Communication involves the sharing of human experiences, ideas, thoughts, opinions, and attitudes with others. This is most easily accomplished when both the sender and receiver of the message are similar. Examples abound of people who are not able to arouse similar meanings within the person to whom they are speaking.

Dr. Paul Watzlawick, well-known communication theorist and psychoanalyst, gives the following example of a communication breakdown. He arrived at a psychiatric research institute for an interview about an assistantship. The following conversation took place between him and the receptionist:

Visitor: Good afternoon, I have an appointment with Dr. H. My name is Watzlawick (vAHT-sla-vick).
Receptionist: I did not say it was.
Visitor: (taken aback and somewhat annoyed): But I am telling you it *is*.
Receptionist: (bewildered) Why then did you say it wasn't?
Visitor: But I *said* it was!

Watzlawick explains that at this point the visitor was "certain" that he was being made the object of some incomprehensible but disrespectful joke, while, as it turned out, the receptionist had by then decided that the visitor must be a new psychotic patient of Dr. H's. Eventually it became clear that instead of "My name is Watzlawick" the receptionist had understood "My name is not Slavic." Thus, when one is not able to arouse shared meaning in another person, the conclusion is often reached that he is "crazy." In much the same way, members of one ethnic group may not be able to arouse shared meaning with another group.

Intercultural communication refers to those aspects of communication that are influenced by cultural differences. This happens when the sender and receiver of the communication or message do not share the same system of beliefs, perceptions, attitudes, and messages for the symbols that are exchanged between them. Since meanings are in people, and not in words, communication difficulties occur when individuals do not share common meanings for the exchanged words.

Cultural distinctions among people should not be threatening. On the contrary, they may be viewed as interesting, exciting, and broadening for those interacting with members of other cultures. Most people do not appreciate the profound phenomenon of cultural differences.

For example, anthropologist Edward Hall points out that it is difficult to conceal our conception of time. By examining the different ethnic concepts of time, one can see how cultural concepts influence people's behavior and communication. The most prevalent concept of time in America is commercial. Our language reflects the importance of "getting there on time," "making up time," "losing time," or the dire consequence of "forgetting the time," and now in our computer age, "real time." Conversely, black Americans tend to have, as Arthur L. Smith phrases it, a more "hang-loose" attitude toward it. This is not to indicate in any way that one concept is more worthy or "right" than the other.

Another example of cultural differences is the use of space.

Each individual surrounds himself with a "bubble of privacy" which he feels is his own space. To an American, a short distance is necessary for this bubble—usually two to three feet. To a German, the distance must be much greater. The German goes to great efforts to preserve his privacy, including keeping his office door closed.

The Englishman has yet another concept of space. While the American uses space to classify people, the Englishman may never have had any space to call his own. However, this does not seem to bother him. Even members of Parliament have no offices but often conduct their interviews in foyers or whatever public place is convenient.

The French people are fairly representative of cultures bordering the Mediterranean. They live, eat, work, and relax in crowds. Having always been surrounded by large numbers of people, they require very small personal space or bubble.

The Arabs get so close during conversations that they tend to breathe on each other. To Arabs smelling each other is a desirable way of communicating, and they take special pains to enhance body odors.

Thus, space is a cultural concept. It is learned and significantly influences the way people behave. Culture affects our interpersonal communication, and by being aware of the various concepts of space and time, the executive can prevent some communication breakdowns.

Jim Hughey and Arlee Johnson divide cultural differences into two categories. The first of these is language differences and the second is value patterns.

When considering language differences, one must include communication between races which both speak a common language such as English. Although the shared language does facilitate communication in many ways, it must be remembered that all cultures do not use the language in the same way. Many people who are bilingual—Chicanos, Puerto Ricans, American Indians— view and use English differently than those who have facility in only one language. Language differences must be considered by the sensitive communicator. If a language is shared, differences still exist in terms of how it is used. These differences often are reflected in people's perceptions of reality.

The second type of cultural differences is value patterns. Cultures, groups, and individuals differ from one another, not because some possess values that the others do not, but rather because some give a greater priority to certain values in given situations, whereas the others have an alternative set of priorities. Hughey and Johnson refer to the distinctive way a culture, group, or individual orders or gives priority to its values as a value pattern.

By understanding the value patterns of a racial or cultural group, one is better able to communicate with them. During the actual communication exchange, information can be learned that will help the listener determine the individual's particular value patterns.

Of course, the individual who frequently engages in conversations with members of various cultural groups becomes more sensitive and successful. How often do you communicate with members of other groups? Hughey and Johnson have developed a Transracial Communication Quotient (TCQ) based on frequency of contact.

You can compute your TCQ by following their method. Think of the conversations lasting more than five minutes that you have had during the past seven days. Using a stopwatch or having someone else time you, take five minutes to write all of the names of black people you have talked with for more than five minutes during the past seven days. Then you have five minutes to list the names of the Chicanos with whom you have conversed. Continue the procedure until you have dealt with all of the racial-cultural groups in which you have come in contact. Be sure to include your own racial-cultural group.

After you have listed the names for all groups, count the number of names and place the appropriate number in the space to the right of each racial-cultural group in the list.

Now compute your own TCQ for each racial-cultural group. The formula is:

$$\text{TCQ} = 100 \times \frac{\text{Number of names for a specific racial-cultural group}}{\text{Number of names for your own racial-cultural group}}$$

Although no norms have yet been established for TCQ, Hughey and Johnson suggest you may want to interpret the TCQ like an IQ score with 100 being normal.

After you have computed TCQ scores for each of the racial-cultural groups on your list, determine the percentage of contacts you have with each racial-cultural group. First, add up all the names you recorded totally. Then divide the number of names for each racial-cultural group by this total number and multiply by 100. For example, if you listed a total of fifty names and if you listed five names from the black racial-cultural group:

$$\text{Percent of Contacts with Blacks} \quad \frac{5}{50} = .10 = 10 \text{ percent}$$

This score should give you an indication of how many conversations you have and with whom. There are probably many cultural groups for which you would have a zero. By being aware of our lack of experience in communicating with individuals from other cultural groups, you can become more sensitive to learning how to communicate with them.

One of the strongest barriers to communicating with minorities is lack of trust. In order to have trust, each of the communicators must have had positive experiences with members of that cultural group previously. We are more likely to believe messages from people whom we feel we can trust.

By being suspicious of the speaker, we are rejecting what he has to say. A statement made by someone whom we consider biased or untrustworthy we do not believe while the same statement made by someone with high credibility we do believe and accept. One research finding related to this came from an experiment in which a speaker was introduced as an M.D. and research specialist in the field of medicine and human affairs. The same person in another setting with a similar group was introduced as a student. There was a lower degree of acceptance of information presented by the "student" than that offered by a "medical specialist," even though the same information was presented to both groups. But the speaker posing as a doctor had more credibility and thus more of his message was believed.

Suspicion or lack of trust hinders the listener's receptivity to the message. If we are talking with a member of a cultural group whom we do not trust, we may likely discredit information from him that we would have accepted had it been given to us by a member of our own racial or cultural group.

Accompanying suspicion or lack of trust is defensive behavior. This may be a nonverbal show of fear, such as stepping backward, looking away, turning sideways, or staring at the floor. It can also be indicated by verbal hesitancies, refusal to give a clear and straightforward answer to a question, or a direct, personal attack.

One behavior that contributes to defensiveness is an appearance of lack of concern for the individual with whom one is speaking. Many believe this air of neutrality contributes to communication, but actually it functions as a barrier. A clinically detached or impersonal manner is resented and sometimes feared, in much the same way as the attitude of superiority.

Unfortunately this failure to accept one another often leads to hostility. There are several levels of hostility and many ways of dealing with it. Some people deny they are hostile while others try to conceal it from the person it is directed against. One thing is certain—hostility within the speaker is conveyed to the listener.

Hostility is usually increased by the response it produces. For example, a female, black employee, Ms. X, was promised by her white, male superior, Mr. Y, that he would do "everything possible" to get her promoted. After two months had passed and Ms. X had received no mention of the possible promotion, she began to feel that she had been deceived. Mr. Y obviously was only putting her off, she reasoned. When she concluded that Mr. Y had no intention of trying to get her the promotion, her attitude changed as did her work habits. After this had continued for a few weeks, Mr. Y called Ms. X into his office and asked what was wrong. She replied with seething hostility, "Nothing." He tried again, "But there must be. Only a few weeks ago we talked about a promotion and your future with the company."

That remark burst the dam of resentment, "What promotion? There's not going to be any promotion. You don't have any intention of promoting me, now or ever!"

Mr. Y began to shout that indeed he did, but quickly realized that such a reaction on his part would only escalate the argument. Instead he sighed loudly, collected his composure, and responded very quietly. "I have kept my promise to try to get you that promotion." He called his secretary and requested, "Bring me all my correspondence on Ms. X's possible promotion."

This action on his part produced enough change in Ms. X's attitude that she appeared to be willing to listen. Mr. Y explained that the company was preparing to introduce a new product and that top administration's attention was on it. He simply had not been able to get them to act on the promotion. He outlined what he had done as well as what he planned to do and when. The difficulty was successfully resolved. Of course, Mr. Y would have been a better communicator if he had kept Ms. X informed of what he was doing as it was occurring, or at least indicated in some way that he was acting on the matter. Also it is evident here of different attitudes toward time. Ms. X was anxious for news about the promotion, whereas Mr. Y was less sensitive to the time element.

When the hostile meeting took place, Mr. Y could have viewed Ms. X's comments as an attack on his integrity, and the hostility would have escalated. Usually hostility produces hostility. Most of us, when we feel the hostility of another person directed at us, respond with hostility. We become alert, prepared to defend ourselves from attack. The result: when hostility is introduced into a conversation or discussion, effective communication ceases.

Another barrier to effective communication with minorities is differing attitudes. In a staff meeting I once attended, a man expressed the belief that a person should only go to work if he "felt like it." Naturally his remark was considered controversial and many present responded with incredulous disbelief. A somewhat heated argument followed and hostility increased.

One member of the group quietly addressed the man by name and asked, "How long have you been with this organization?" "Five years," came the reply. "What has been your average number of days absent during those five years?" The man answered, "About one day a year."

The group members suddenly realized that the man's absentee record was, in many cases, better than theirs. The man was voicing a different attitude and his listeners were demonstrating a typical response, intolerance and closemindedness. Too often the listener fails to set aside his own attitudes and thus understand what the other person's position is and why.

Studies indicate that the point in time when an opinion is acquired ultimately affects the rigidity with which it is held. Time may cause an opinion to become more vulnerable. This does not mean that the person holds an opinion with any less firmness after passage of time, but the longer he has held the opinion, the greater the likelihood that he will listen to contrary ideas.

The recent convert is the hardest person to convince because he will not really hear what is actually said. The more the content of the message is characterized by judgment or inference, the more the convert will challenge it. By jumping to conclusions, deciding what is to be said before it is said, the listener never receives the total message.

Inadequate sensitivity is regarded as another important barrier to communication. This may be the barrier which is most frequently cited by members of minority groups. The individual who cannot perceive or accurately sense what the other may feel or think or do is not sensitive to communication. We have all experienced incidents when someone obviously embarrassed and possibly humiliated another person because of a lack of sensitivity. Perhaps what made us so uncomfortable was that the individual could not see what he was doing to the other person. A warning goes off in one's head which says, "If he will do it to him, he may unknowingly do it to me."

The higher the position in the organization the offender holds, the greater the offense. A conference was sponsored by a large organization, and the president presided over the luncheon. Dessert was orange sherbet. To most of us such a selection is often what accompanies these meals, but to the president of that organization it represented a colossal staff mistake. He began his address by apologizing to all the men present for having orange sherbet. He continued, "Everyone knows that sherbet is only for women."

When the sprinkling of women in the audience began to squirm in their seats, the president smiled and added, "I'm sure you women enjoyed it, but, believe me, we men didn't."

By now everyone was equally uncomfortable but the matter was not over yet. He named the staff person, a woman, who had been responsible for overseeing the conference. Directing his final comment to her he sternly instructed, "I'm sure in the future she will be able to remember not to order orange sherbet." The obvious discomfort of the woman was totally ignored by the president who finally began his discussion of the announced topic. The woman, an intelligent college graduate who, no doubt, has hated orange sherbet since that day, soon went to work for a competitor whom she believed would be more appreciative of her skills.

Stories of the incident circulated among the firm's female employees for weeks. Many took it as an indication of the president's chauvinistic attitude, and the total negative effect of his careless remarks is probably incalculable.

John W. Keltner points out that a nice balance of sensitivity—neither too much nor too little—contributes much to effective communication. A person who is himself exceptionally sensitive may not be able to communicate with someone who is less sensitive. This individual may assume the listener has skills to pick up subtle indications that he is not capable of perceiving. In order for the highly sensitive communicator to make himself understood, he may have to build in details for the less sensitive listener or receiver.

THE EITHER-OR SYNDROME

Another barrier to communication is the either-or syndrome. Unfortunately most things are not simple. It is not easy to know what the "truth" is because we have seen how a person's perceptions determine how and what they see. Thus, right/wrong, good/bad extremes do not exist, but rather there is some right and some wrong. Most actions, beliefs, and attitudes are subject to many shades of meaning and interpretation.

At the initial meeting of contract negotiations, management offered to hire a certain percent of its workers from minority groups. After presenting the proposal, the company representative stated that the union could either accept it or reject it, but that there would be no alternatives. The union representative quickly retorted, "If that's the way you want it to be, I reject it." Most negotiations proceed to the stage of modifying and generating other possibilities until an agreement is reached. Too rigid an interpretation of alternatives only blocks routes to compromise.

UNWARRANTED ASSUMPTIONS

Making unwarranted assumptions based on previous experience also contributes to communication breakdowns. Particularly when talking with members of minority groups, one tends to generalize and make unwarranted assumptions. The personnel director who refers to knowing how to handle someone because he has "dealt with his kind before" is certainly headed for trouble. Communication difficulties begin with treating an individual the same as we have another individual because they are of the same race. Often that is all they have in common.

Arthur L. Smith gives this example of how we generalize when we learn someone's race. A teacher with predominantly Caucasian characteristics got a position in a California high school. She was an excellent teacher, and no one at the predominantly white school gave or expressed a thought about her being of any other race. One day she made this comment about fair housing, "As a black woman, I feel that we must protect the right of every person to own or rent a home anywhere he wants." The room fell silent. Afterwards she was treated with great coolness by her colleagues. Efforts to communicate now had an additional element—she was black—and her fellow teachers began to converse with her on a different basis. Smith notes that the woman eventually became the sociologist, economist, and commentator on all black-related events. Whereas before she had simply given her opinion like others, now her communication was interpreted from a different perspective.

A number of communication barriers have been discussed. Certainly all have not been included, just those which seem to hinder effective communication between members of different cultural groups. Lack of trust, defensive behavior, hostility, differing attitudes, inadequate sensitivity, the either-or syndrome, and making unwarranted assumptions are the biggest barriers. By being aware of these difficulties one can try to avoid them, but there are also a number of bridges the sensitive communicator can use to improve his communication with members of various cultural groups.

Bridges to Communicating with Minorities

You begin with trust. If you want others to trust you, you must first indicate to them your acceptance, warmth, and empathy. Communication between people is based on trust. By focusing on trust, you soon see that the person is relying upon another person to help achieve some goal or gain. Although some potential loss is risked, the potential gain, if his trust is warranted, is greater.

Establishing trust between people leads to decreased suspicion and increased tolerance for behavior that is "unusual." Positive interaction between people produces more positive interaction. As one becomes comfortable talking with members of other minorities, the trusting relationship leads to other attempts at communicating.

Another bridge to improved communication is accurate perception. To perceive refers not only to seeing similarities in people, but perhaps more important, to seeing differences. Everything changes over time and so too should our perceptions. Just as you are not now the person you were five years ago or even one year ago, so too should our perceptions be updated. One example of this is the "radicals" of the sixties who are now engaged in many so-called establishment activities. By avoiding once-and-for-all decisions, we become able to perceive more accurately.

When you are considering communication with minorities, it is important to realize that perceptions about a racial group often hinder communication. Until preconceived notions are put aside, there is little communication actually taking place. The black who perceives all whites as vicious and racist will communicate that stereotyped perspective. Fortunately, new facts often do change attitudes, and stereotypes give way to more accurate perceptions.

A second bridge to effective communication with minorities is the unconditional positive regard for the other person. This, of course, is not easily accomplished, mainly because we are all prejudiced. This process of positively regarding the other person is increased if the other person has some status or if his behavior satisfies some immediate and important personal need. Hence, the minority person needs to be given the opportunity to demonstrate competency.

Another bridge is empathic understanding. By trying to see the world through the eyes of the beholder rather than your own viewpoint, you demonstrate acceptance of the other person. You permit him his separateness and indicate that you do not expect him to be like you. You come to appreciate others for their being, their uniqueness, and subsequently learn from those who are different, rather than being threatened by them.

Only when people relate to people can communication occur. Unlike physical growth which comes without conscious effort on our part, the growth of understanding requires both effort and risk. We must exert extra effort to be open and understanding and by doing so lay aside our cultural blindfolds.

Smith has identified two influences which he considers to be the most crucial on transracial communication. These are "willingness and availability." He explains willingness by noting that the potential communicator is not indifferent to the communication event, but is actively interested in what is being communicated by the source of the message. Implied in this willingness is an attempt to become accessible to the other person. Smith states that physical proximity is only one part of accessibility. The other is the flexibility and sensitivity of the two persons. If they are in physical proximity and are sensitive to each other—able to anticipate responses, attitudes and judgments—then "real" availability exists. What is said and how it is taken depend on willingness and availability.

Another bridge to communication is the ability to distinguish fact from opinion. In the organizational environment statements of opinion are often mistakenly taken as statements of fact. If one minority spokesman expresses his views, what he says should be considered opinion, not fact. Opinions are meaningful as long as they are identified and understood to be what they are, opinions. If we began every statement of opinion by preceding it with "I think" or "I believe" probably most of our statements would be prefaced with that phrase. When making important policy decisions, the administrator should know that it is particularly important that opinion be distinguished from fact. In a large plant in the Midwest an assembly line change was planned. The administrators asked two of the minority members who worked there if the changes would be acceptable to them. The two responded that they would. However, when the changes were introduced, several problems developed. The administrators had assumed that because the two workers had said the changes were acceptable that all of the other minority workers would find them acceptable. Such an assumption was unjustified. If the top administrators wanted to know how all employees would react, they should have asked all or taken a scientific sample of opinions.

Too often a minority spokesman emerges who is not a legitimate spokesman at all. The administrators choose a minority member whom they consider nonthreatening, but this person, due to the same characteristic that attracted management to him, may be totally unacceptable to minority members. Every effort should be made to separate fact from opinion, and when one is dealing with opinions, care should be taken about generalizing from one person's opinion to the entire group.

Another consideration in evaluating information is to determine how many people filtered the information before it was relayed. Years ago a popular indoor game was "Gossip." It consisted of players sitting in a circle and one person whispering a statement to the person on his right who repeated it to the person on his right, and on and on. The last person to get the message had to repeat it aloud, and the originator announced what he had actually said. The two statements usually bore little resemblance to each other.

In an organization this same type of communication distortion happens every day. There can be no other explanation for some of the distortions that occur. At each transfer station (the person who receives and retransmits the message) some of the message is lost, and perhaps something is added or reshaped. The more stations involved in the transmission of the message, the greater the distortion. A decision made to economize, transferred down through the organization may well reach the rank and file, such as a decision to lay off hundreds of workers. For example, the management of an organization in financial difficulty decided not to replace employees who resigned. As the story spread through the organization, this decision was interpreted as one aimed at eliminating minority employees.

Feedback can be used as a bridge to communicating with members of minority groups. Feedback is time-consuming, threatening, and troublesome. But despite these 3 Ts feedback remains the most important block to building good communication. Whereas the subordinate has only one person to worry about, the boss, the superior has many subordinates to worry about. A remark innocently made to some of them may not cause any trouble but to others it may be completely misinterpreted.

I once attended a company meeting on affirmative action programs. The white employees left the meeting convinced that the administrators meant exactly what they said about increasing the number of minority employees working for the company. However, on the way back to my office I overheard several minority employees agreeing that things were not to change at all and concluding that the meeting was nothing but window dressing. Meanwhile, the president, convinced that he had "communicated," decided that the topic did not need to be discussed again. What was needed was a feedback loop. A feedback loop would have told the president that the message he had sent was not received as he had intended. His assumption that he had communicated, when in reality he had not, was as dangerous as not having tried at all!

How does the administrator indicate his desire for feedback? By encouraging people to speak up, disagree, and question. However, it is not enough to say you want feedback; how you react when you get feedback is just as important. The director of a not-for-profit organization told all of his new employees that his door was "always open," and that any topic they were concerned about could always be talked over with him. However, when an employee tested his statement, the director leaned back in his chair, looked out the window, and suggested that the employee should work such a small matter out for himself. The open-door policy and desire for feedback were in name only. This is not to say that the director was purposefully misleading his employees; quite the contrary, he did genuinely mean what he had said. But he could not see that he was "turning off" anyone who tried to follow through on what he said.

This same misunderstanding frequently occurs between communicators who are members of different cultural groups. To tell employees you want feedback may not be enough. Although that is the first step, it is only that, the first step. Additionally one must identify the subjects on which you particularly want feedback, provide opportunity for feedback and, most importantly, reward feedback.

The subjects on which you want feedback should be selected on the basis of what one needs to know to run the organization more effectively. By providing certain opportunities for feedback, times and places, the administrator improves the likelihood of getting feedback. By simply letting minority members know that an opportunity is being given them, you have done much to establish good relations. It should be made clear that this invitation for feedback is not to be a session for name calling, but a sincere effort to improve relations between the administration and the minority employees.

Rewards for feedback should be given. These need not be monetary but could be oral or written recognition. Another means of rewarding feedback is to take action on the information received and make certain that the minority member is informed of it.

In conclusion, there are a number of ways the administrator can build bridges to communicating with minorities. Establishing trust is important as are accurate perceptions. If the administrator has a positive regard for the other person and uses empathic understanding, communication can occur. Willingness and availability are the two conditions which must be established.

Caution must be taken to distinguish fact from opinion and to consider how many "transfer stations" the information passed through. Lastly, feedback can be used to establish good communication, but it must be actively sought, opportunities provided and rewarded.

THE CONFRONTATION MEETING

Richard Beckhard has described the confrontation meeting, a method recommended for times of stress or major change. In this meeting information on problems and attitudes is collected and fed back to those who produced it, and steps are taken to start action plans for improvement of the condition. Any organization may have a very short period of time between identifying the problem and determining a course of action. The confrontation meeting can be carried out in four and a half to five hours working time, and it is designed to include the entire management of a large system in a joint action-planning program.

Although Beckhard described the confrontation meeting as used by top management for resolving internal difficulties, it can also be used to resolve problems with minority groups. The head of a Department of State office had hundreds of angry blacks invade his office building. The departmental head had been completely insensitive to communicating, and in exasperation the black leaders had decided to demonstrate their frustrations.

While the mass media interviewed black leaders, the governmental officials huddled and debated what to do. Finally the departmental head, Mr. A, sent out word that he would meet with a few leaders only and discuss their grievances. The leaders responded by having all of their followers shout a loud "NO!" Later, after negotiations between the two sides, it was agreed that a meeting would be held between Mr. A and the black leaders, but it would take place in a large auditorium where all demonstrators could see and hear the proceedings.

The leaders outlined the magnitude of the problem. Mr. A divided the topic into several areas based on the organizational structure of his department. He had each of his top administrators for each of the areas meet with leaders for two hours. They were told to get specifics and indicate what resources were available to address each of the needs.

When the total group met again, each of the subgroups gave a report. Certain action was agreed to along with a timetable for it. Additionally, possible future actions were outlined along with a timetable for deciding them. All the actions were listed by priority.

By the end of the day, only five hours after the demonstration had begun, the leaders left with a list of what action was to be taken and when, what additional action was to be considered and when the decisions were to be made, and what follow-up action would be taken to insure they would not have to resort to demonstrations to get the administrators' attention.

A confrontation meeting in this case was the result of communication failures. Confrontation meetings can be called by administrators when they are having difficulty getting feedback on a problem. If designed to follow Beckhard's structure these meetings can be productive. These are:

1. Climate setting—establishing willingness to participate (about forty-five minutes to one hour).
2. Information collecting—getting the attitudes and feelings out in the open (one hour).
3. Information sharing—making total information available to all (one hour).
4. Priority setting and group action planning—holding work-unit sessions to set priority actions and to make timetable commitments (one hour and fifteen minutes).
5. Organization action planning—getting commitment by top management to meeting these priorities (one to two hours).
6. Immediate follow-up by the top management committee—planning first actions and commitments (one to three hours).

According to Beckhard the confrontation meeting produces several positive results. A high degree of open communication is achieved quickly. The information collected is current and correct. It provides a format for a real dialogue between the top management team and the rest of the organization. Increased trust and confidence are produced.

Although the confrontation meeting is usually considered as an effective tool for times of stress or major change, it can also be used for improving communication with members of minority groups.

The Importance of Effective Communication with Minorities

Psychologists have stated that we are what we have experienced. By the very definition of being members of a minority group, those of us who are not could never share some of the experiences which these individuals have had. In much the same way, the members of one minority group may not be able to relate to the experiences of another minority group because the cultural differences between a black and a white may be no greater than those of a black and a Chicano.

Since these cultural differences do exist, particular efforts must be made to become aware of the barriers they erect, and communication knowledge must be used to break through them. The effectiveness of an organization depends on the effectiveness of its communication with all its employees. Regardless of what level minority members occupy within the organization, management or rank and file, the sensitive communicator realizes that difficulties may be encountered because of a difference in using culturalbound symbols and signs. This is not to imply a good/bad, right/wrong judgment. Rather it is to point out that communication has to be tailored to the individual. This is just as true of the minority as of the majority cultural member. Improved communication begins with awareness, because meanings are in people, not just words.

10

ASSESSING THE COMMUNICATION CLIMATE OF YOUR ORGANIZATION

The talented administrator knows that he does not know all there is to know.

Unknown

There has recently been a new awareness of the importance of effective communication as an essential function of an organization. When communication begins to fall apart, organizational goals of efficiency, productivity, and profit are sure to decline. Additionally, communication breakdowns, by frustrating those who take their jobs seriously, can also lead to a general decrease in morale.

Top management has always initiated studies or analyses to determine organizational problem areas. Communication was excluded completely or included only as a secondary element. A systematic, thorough evaluation of the organization's communication climate was never undertaken. However, a technique—the communication audit—has been recently developed which may be successfully used to conduct just such an evaluation.

The communication audit evaluates the effectiveness of communication systems and activities within the organization. The technique allows for the special characteristics of each organization by permitting the consultant to tailor the audit to the organization's specific needs.

Planning the Communication Audit

A communication audit is usually conducted by a consultant trained in organization communication. The consultant and management representatives establish the objectives of the audit. These could include: assessing the effectiveness of the organizational communication system; mapping the communication flows within the organization; identifying weak areas in the communication system; determining if appropriate elements for a good system are missing; making recommendation for correction of apparent deficiencies; and planning for increased communication effectiveness.

The audit generally evaluates horizontal, upward, and downward communication along with the grapevine and formal and informal communication networks. By setting the objectives for the audit, the consultant and management determine which specific areas within the organization are to be studied and by what instrument and methods. The number and types of employees to be studied often dictate which particular method the communication audit team will use.

Selection of the Instruments

Although many instruments can be used in a communication audit, most are one of three major types of data gathering techniques: the questionnaire, the interview, and observation.

The wide use of the questionnaire has made it familiar to almost everyone. It is a written instrument which attempts to get information on attitudes, knowledge, and perceptions on a particular subject, topic, or activity. The identity of the individual completing the form usually remains anonymous. Auditors like to use the questionnaire because it is administered easily, costs little, and takes little time. It can be used to obtain a wide variety of information.

The interview, also used by the auditor, is more versatile, allowing the auditor to get follow-up information, and in-depth comments. By actually talking with the individual, the auditor can get feedback on attitudes, beliefs, and perceptions.

Observation is the third methodology used in the communication audit. The phases of this technique are: observing, recording, and analyzing. The main advantages of the observation technique are the flexibility and the opportunity to question the individual about his behavior as soon as it occurs.

Conclusions of the Communication Audit

After analyzing the data, the auditor looks for patterns, familiar elements, relationships, and trends which indicate the state of communication effectiveness. This information is compared to the optimal state of the organization as derived from the statement of objectives. The comparison requires the auditor to look at the data he has collected and the conclusions he has drawn from them with the statements made by the organizational representatives regarding the desired state.

If the present state and optimal state are not the same, the auditor makes recommendations on corrective action. By drawing on his experience, knowledge, and training, he proposes specific actions which can be taken to alleviate certain communication problems.

WHY THE COMMUNICATION AUDIT?

A regular review of an organization's communication climate will identify problem areas and missed opportunities. The communication audit can be accomplished quickly and can be tailored to the needs of the specific organization—either one part or the entire organization.

A communication audit answers such questions as: What is the overall communication climate of the organization? Are employee relations communication objectives being met? How cost-effective is the current communication program? Is there an ongoing communication evaluation program? What type of interpersonal relations exist among top management? Is the communication program an integral part of the organization?

The typical communication audit gets input from at least four levels of the organization: the chief executive, the top personnel manager or communication administrator, a representative from each major area, and rank-and-file employees.

The information elicited from the chief executive focuses on his views for effective internal and external communication. The executive's evaluation of his current program is considered as is his role in it. Any ideas or plans for changing the program are discussed.

On the second level, the top personnel manager or communication administrator is asked for formal, written communication objectives and policies. If there are none, the person is asked to propose what the key ones are. The method of establishing priorities is studied as is the overall communication plan and budget. The programs which are considered most effective are identified as are those considered least effective. Methods of evaluation are detailed along with any use of outside assistance in the communication program. The administrator is asked to identify methods which have an upward, downward, and horizontal flow.

Managers who represent different areas are asked if they feel informed about plans and developments. The amount of cooperation between departments is assessed along with the amount of information they need to make daily decisions. These midlevel administrators can be asked to tell how they communicate with their people or how they feel about management's efforts to establish effective upward channels of communication.

The rank-and-file employees are asked if the organization does a good job of keeping them informed of its plans and developments. Other questions establish how they feel about the way employee complaints are handled and if they get satisfactory answers to their questions from their supervisors.

The audit asks these and many, many other questions depending on what the consultant and management have set as their objectives. The audit can be for the entire organization, for only a part of it, or for a particularly troublesome aspect, for example, feelings and attitudes on the need for communication training.

The communication audit will tell the administrator certain information about his organization. For example, Company C had a team of auditors assess its communication climate. The findings showed that: downward communication at the supervisor level was poor; that middle managers sought much information from informal sources as they found it more reliable, current, and easier to obtain; that top management complained that their midlevel people would not tell them of trouble until it was at the crisis stage; and that foremen particularly felt left out of the flow of information, complaining that information was always withheld from them until the last possible moment.

A communication audit report includes not only the findings but also suggested recommendations. In addition to the types of problems in the organization and the depth of the concerns, the auditors recommend policies and changes which will aid the organization in performing more effectively. Thus, a communication audit is a first step in putting together a plan for improved management through communication.

Audits can focus on various aspects of the organization. This is important because in many organizations communication functions are handled by many different departments or divisions. Some responsibility is often in Public Relations, Personnel, and perhaps Community Relations. The audit is flexible, functioning as an evaluation tool in any one area, or on a more general level such as identifying communication networks in an organization.

COMMUNICATION NETWORKS

Networks or patterns of communication occur in all organizations. It is tempting to believe that only formal organizational charts depict communication channels in an organization, but this is not true. Informal networks can just as easily become structured and continue over time. A communication audit can be used to study the networks in an organization.

Communication networks are built on the communication linkages between persons in an organization. By focusing on the exchange of messages, the auditor can identify a number of different networks.

For example, an administrator could build a communication network based on the frequency of contact, weekly, daily, or several times a day. One could construct a network according to different kinds of communication content. One network could map communications having to do with production—getting the job done. Another could focus on communications having to do with relationships—personnel problems, group identities, morale, and cohesiveness of the work force. Finally a communication network could be plotted that would measure communications having to do with change—innovations, organizational development, and planning.

A third way of constructing communication networks for an organization could be based on the communication channels, such as memos, distribution lists, letters, and phoning. This type of network is useful to the organization for determining the most effective way of getting a message across to all employees or a particular group.

WHY DO A NETWORK ANALYSIS?

The primary goal of network analysis is to identify the particular channels through which communication flows in an organization. By achieving this goal the administrator through network analysis can describe the ongoing, day-to-day communication patterns in his/her organization.

Since the network analysis provides a "map" of actual or real communication patterns (exchanged messages) a comparison can be made with the formal organizational chart. If the observed communication deviates from the formal (proposed or expected), an administrator can tell to what extent and precisely where the deviation occurs. In short, the network analysis can tell where the communication problems are.

Once the network is complete, communication groups can be identified. Such knowledge is valuable. With this information an administrator can identify those groups that are isolated, or too dominated by one or two individuals. He/she can spot those groups that are too large or too small.

Some groups may be too highly connected to others suggesting information overload while others may have too many gatekeepers slowing or distorting the information to them. The more links in the communication channel the greater the chance of information distortion. The linkages between groups should also tell an administrator the fastest way to get a message through the organization by identifying the most direct route.

IDENTIFYING A COMMUNICATION NETWORK

Communication networks are simply regular patterns of communication between people in an organization. Regular exchanges result from talking face-to-face, phoning one another and exchanging memos, but such networks of communication are essential since they provide the basic structure or informal organizational chart by which information is exchanged throughout the organization.

The human nervous system is a helpful analogy of the communication networks in an organization. In the human body, the nervous system carries information between the various parts of the body and makes it possible for the whole system to function. In an organization the communication network performs a similar function in that information is exchanged between people allowing the entire organizational system to perform.

In essence, organizations are made up of people who perform various roles. The linkages between people (the "nerves") are communication channels. Because these linkages are established and maintained, it is possible to examine an organization and find recurring patterns of communication exchange. In short, it is possible to map the "nervous system" (communication networks) of an organization because certain groups of people will engage in communication with one another on a regular basis. Therefore, by mapping the patterns of communication between the people in the organization, we can identify groups of individuals who communicate frequently with one another, thus forming the communication network of the organization.

Usually administrators are somewhat familiar with the idea of communication networks. To develop or use an organizational chart, a formal communication network depicting the appropriate channels for communication exchange, i.e., decisions, instructions, and memos, is one level of awareness. Most administrators are also aware that members of the organization often form their own informal organizational chart, communication networks that don't follow the prescribed formal channels, i.e., the grapevine.

Effective administrators develop a feel for the various kinds of communication networks that exist in their shops. However, such an intuitive feeling for the informal networks may be biased, often limited, or even wrong. Often such an intuitive feeling tells the administrator that communication patterns differ from the formal, or what they expect to occur, but that this feeling does not tell one how large the deviation is, nor does it pinpoint exactly where the deviation occurs. Network analysis can provide this information.

CONDUCTING A NETWORK ANALYSIS

A network analysis begins with acquiring or making a formal organizational chart. For our purposes we will construct one for our hypothetical organization, M. This is shown in Figure 1. Our organization will have nineteen people. Our formal organizational chart shows three major divisions within the organization. The numbers within the blocks represent persons, with person 1 in charge of the entire organization and persons 2, 3, and 4 serving as supervisors of Divisions One, Two, and Three, respectively. The remaining numbers (5–19) represent the various employees of the three divisions

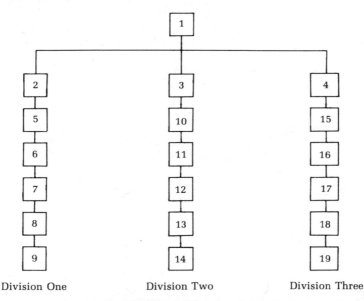

Division One   Division Two   Division Three

Figure 1. The Organizational Chart of Organization M

Our next step in identifying a communication network is to develop a questionnaire that will reveal the communication relationships within the organization. To do this, we ask each employee via the questionnaire to indicate his frequency of communication with each employee in the organization. In our example for Organization M, every employee would be given a list of nineteen names and asked to indicate how often he communicates with each person on a work day using a scale from "almost never" to "several times a day." These responses can be quantified so as to construct a score for each employee.

After collecting these communication data through the questionnaire, we can analyze it for any frequency of contact—almost never to several times a day. For our purposes here, we will select the frequency, "several times a day," to construct our communication network.

All nineteen persons, based on hypothetical data obtained from our questionnaire, are shown graphically in Figure 2. Individuals in Organization M are indicated by placing their person numbers within a circle. These are called communication nodes and the communicative connection between any two people represented by a line called a *link*. All nineteen employees are represented and links have been drawn to illustrate communication contacts at the frequency of "several times a day." This graphic format, Figure 2, makes it possible to map a communication network that would not be possible by examining each questionnaire individually.

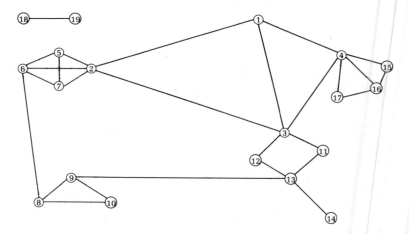

Figure 2. Communication Link Network between Employees of Organization M

Now that we have our basic communication network, we can analyze it for additional information. This is possible by constructing a classification scheme that describes the communication network roles filled by the people of Organization M. Examine Figure 3. Notice that we have several clusters or groups of people. These are called communication *groups* because they consist of three or more people having at least 50 percent of their contacts with each other. The percentage of contacts is obtained from our original questionnaire. Based on our hypothetical data we can see which clusters of people actually form our communication groups A, B, C, and D. These groups are shown in Figure 3.

Now that we have identified our communication groups, we can point out a second type of communication role—the *bridge*. This is a person that connects the various communication groups. In Figure 3, persons (clockwise) 4, 3, 13, 9, 8, 6, and 2 occupy bridge roles because they link groups in their communicative activity.

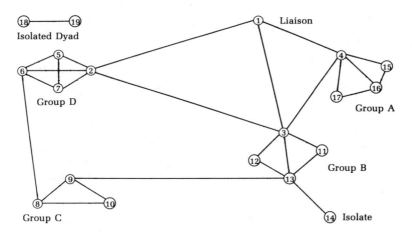

Figure 3. Communication Link Network between Employees of Organization M

One of the most important communication roles identified in Figure 3 is the liaison or person 1. In communication network analysis, a *liaison* is the person who does not share a majority of communication contacts with the members of a single group, but who links two or more groups together. In Figure 3, person 1 is a liaison who has communication links to three different groups.

A final communication role identified by network analysis is that of the isolate. An *isolate* is a person who does not substantially, at some specified frequency level, participate in the communication network. In Figure 3, persons 18, 19, and 14 are isolates.

EVALUATING THE COMMUNICATION NETWORK

Now that a communication network has been identified in our Organization M, it is time to evaluate it and see what implications it has for our organization.

This is best done by superimposing the communication network groupings over the formal organizational chart (Figure 1). In Figure 4 we have drawn the original organizational chart, but have coded the numbers of the members of our four communication groups in the network (Figure 3). For example, we have identified person 15 as being a member of Group A. Now we can also identify person 15's place in our formal organizational chart and also point out Group A's hierarchical location in Organization M. See Figure 4.

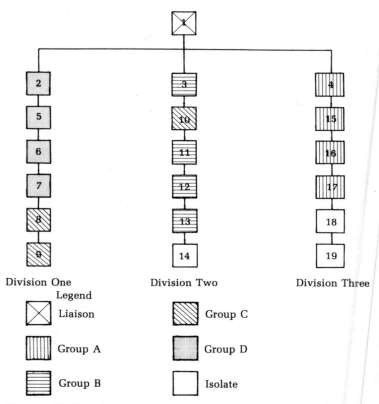

Division One   Division Two   Division Three

Legend

⊠ Liaison   ▨ Group C

▥ Group A   ▦ Group D

▤ Group B   ☐ Isolate

Figure 4. The Four Communication Groups of the Network within Organization M

Group A consists of persons 4, 15, 16, and 17 and is found in Division Three. But Division Three has two other members, persons 18 and 19, according to our formal organizational chart. From Figure 4 it is evident these persons are isolates. Thus we have a communication problem in Division Three in that it has two individuals who appear to be isolated, that is, not communicating with others in their division. Certainly this finding by our network analysis could be used by an administrator to make changes for improving the effectiveness of Division Three.

Communication Group B was comprised of persons 3, 11, 12, and 13 all of whom are found in Division Two. This is fine until we see that Division Two also contains two other members, persons 10 and 14. Person 14 is classified as an isolate, but Person 10 is a member of another communication group—Group C. So Division Two has some of its members who function as a communication isolate or conduct most of their communication activity with members of another division.

Group C's communication is erratic. Two of its members (8, 9) are from Division One and one member (Person 10) is from Division Two. This communication group does not fit our organizational hierarchy. Such a pattern often means that a redrawing of the formal organizational chart may be needed. Shouldn't this group be placed under the same division or supervisor?

Communication Group D (persons 2, 5, 6, 7) is consistent with the organizational hierarchy since all members are found in Division One.

Our analysis, by superimposing the communication network on the formal organizational chart of Organization M, has revealed some interesting and heretofore unknown patterns. We have found some unexpected groupings according to divisions and identified some isolated individuals. We can point out the persons serving as bridges between groups. Also Person 1 has emerged as the only liaison in our organization. This has important implications if we remember that all of his communication linkages are to his three division heads. This means that Group C, which is not recognized by the formal organizational chart, is then cut off from direct communication with the top administrator, Person 1. Note that all liaisons are not always high in the organization. A liaison may appear at any level in the organizational structure.

In addition Organization M on the basis of this analysis might want to rethink its formal organizational chart to create a more functional environment for Group C. Also because three of the nineteen employees are isolated, communication channels to these persons need to be improved.

IMPLICATIONS FOR ADMINISTRATORS

A network analysis can tell the administrator a great deal about the communicative behavior of the individuals in his/her organization. For example, the network analysis will identify those persons occupying the roles of bridge, liaison and isolate.

Those individuals identified as isolates need to be examined further. Is it the nature of their job that they communicate very little with the other employees, or are they a behavioral problem? Isolates can be a source of communication breakdown and even more so if they remain unknown. Network analysis will identify them.

Employees who fill the roles of bridge and liaison need to be examined by administrators. It may be that you have a person filling this role that should not. For example, a person with inadequate knowledge or training serving as an important link between two technical work groups could likely cause messages to get garbled.

In looking at the entire organization, an administrator will likely increase communication effectiveness if the linkage between groups is made by liaisons rather than bridges. Likert suggests this with his ideas on "linking pins." This is logical in that if a message is to travel to all groups and it can only do this by first going to Group 1 and then Group 2 and finally ending at the last group there is a greater chance for information distortion because of the many links (bridges) in the communication channel. But if that same message went from one liaison to all groups at once, because of fewer links the channel is more direct, and communication breakdown is avoided since all groups should receive the same message from the same source (the liaison).

For the administrator considering change in the organization, network analysis is a valuable tool. Armed with a clear map of the communication patterns in the organization, changes which restructure the old system can be based on fact rather than myth. Since problem areas have been brought to the surface, an administrator has a good idea of what needs to be changed. After the changes have been implemented, an evaluation can be made as to the effectiveness of these structural changes.

A final effective use of network analysis as a management tool is in the area of organizational crisis. For example, if a crisis should envelop the organization, such as an economic cutback or approaching deadlines for final reports or proposals, certain groups may need to communicate more effectively. A network analysis would reveal who is doing what during the crisis situation. Organizations tend to follow the same patterns when dealing with a crisis and a network analysis would reveal this. Once revealed, an administrator can make a more thorough analysis of the crisis management system.

Some organizational theorists argue that to understand a modern organization is to locate the crucial linkages that connect large numbers of the employees. This is precisely what network analysis does.

The important point is not that one administrator rules; rather it is his/her knowledge that administration is made possible by the patterns of relationships that exist between persons in the organization.

The Communication Climate of an Organization

Today's organizations function through communication. Since the communication climate of an organization determines how effectively it functions, social scientists have developed a number of techniques for evaluating that climate. Commonly referred to as the communication audit, the consultant views communication as a management tool. The communication audit technique provides a sophisticated approach for determining communication effectiveness.

The communication audit can be used to determine the characteristics of several aspects of organizational communication. One of these is the informal communication networks which exist in every organization. These networks are simply regular patterns of communication between people in the organization. It is through these networks that organizational goals are achieved or frustrated.

The capable manager or administrator should be aware of what the communication climate of his organization is, not what he thinks it is. The way to get this crucial information is by a systematic, scientific communication audit. This feedback should be solicited regularly and repeatedly to keep management alert to communication problems and the status of the organization's climate.

INDEX